Bryan E Metzger 3/4/97

Other titles in the Jossey-Bass Nonprofit Sector Series:

Achieving Excellence in Fund Raising, *Henry A. Rosso and Associates*

The Board Member's Guide to Fund Raising, *Fisher Howe*

Boards That Make a Difference, *John Carver*

Conducting a Successful Capital Campaign, *Kent E. Dove*

The Corporate Contributions Handbook, *James P. Shannon, Editor*

The Drucker Foundation Self-Assessment Tool for Nonprofit Organizations, *The Peter F. Drucker Foundation for Nonprofit Management*

Effective Fund Raising in Higher Education, *Magaret A. Duronio, Bruce A. Loessin*

Executive Leadership in Nonprofit Organizations, *Robert D. Herman, Richard D. Heimovics*

Governing, Leading, and Managing Nonprofit Organizations, *Dennis R. Young, Virginia A. Hodgkinson, Robert M. Hollister, and Associates*

The Jossey-Bass Handbook of Nonprofit Leadership and Management, *Robert D. Herman and Associates*

Improving Corporate Donations, *Vic Murray*

Leadership and Management of Volunteer Programs, *James C. Fisher, Kathleen M. Cole*

The Makings of a Philanthropic Fundraiser, *Ronald Alan Knott*

New Directions for Philanthropic Fundraising (quarterly journal)

Nonprofit Management and Leadership (quarterly journal)

Principles of Professional Fundraising, *Joseph R. Mixer*

Reinventing Fundraising, *Sondra C. Shaw, Martha A. Taylor*

The Seven Faces of Philanthropy, *Russ A. Prince, Karen A. File*

Strategic Planning for Fund Raising, *Wesley E. Lindahl*

Strategic Planning for Public and Nonprofit Organizations, *John M. Bryson*

Taking Fund Raising Seriously, *Dwight F. Burlingame, Lamont J. Hulse, Editors*

Understanding Nonprofit Funding, *Kirsten A. Grønbjerg*

Women and Power in the Nonprofit Sector, *Teresa Odendahl, Michael O'Neill, Editors*

Winning Grants
Step by Step

Support Centers of America

written by Mim Carlson

Winning Grants Step by Step

Support Centers of America's Complete
Workbook for Planning, Developing, and
Writing Successful Proposals

 Jossey-Bass Publishers • San Francisco

Substantial discounts on bulk quantities of Jossey-Bass books are available to corporations, professional associations, and other organizations. For details and discount information, contact the special sales department at Jossey-Bass Inc., Publishers.

(415) 433–1740; Fax (800) 605–2665.

For sales outside the United States, please contact your local Simon & Schuster International Office. Manufactured in the United States of America.

Library of Congress Cataloging-in-Publication Data

Carlson, Mim, date.
    Winning grants step by step : Support Centers of America's
complete workbook for planning, developing, and writing successful
proposals / Support Centers of America ; written by Mim Carlson.
       p. cm.—(The Jossey-Bass nonprofit sector series)
    Includes bibliographical references.
    ISBN 0-7879-0118-0 (pbk. : alk. paper)
    1. Proposal writing for grants.   2. Nonprofit organizations—
Finance.   I. Support Centers of America (Organization)   II. Title.
III. Series.
HG177.C374   1995
658.15'224 — dc20
                                    95-16793
                                    CIP

FIRST EDITION
PB Printing 10 9 8 7 6 5 4 3 2

The Jossey-Bass
Nonprofit Sector Series

Contents

Acknowledgments

This workbook was developed by the Support Centers of America (SCA) to help staff and volunteers write better, more powerful, and more convincing grant proposals. The Support Centers of America is a national network devoted to increasing the effectiveness of nonprofit organizations. This purpose is accomplished through the delivery of management training, information, and consulting programs—all specifically targeted to and focused on the needs of nonprofits. Each year, Support Centers from coast to coast assist thousands of nonprofit organizations with their management and fundraising needs. This workbook was a product of our experience working with nonprofit staff and volunteers in the area of fundraising and, more specifically, grantwriting. After two decades of offering workshops, clinics, and consultation on the art of proposal writing, we decided something else was needed. *Winning Grants Step by Step* is that something else. We believe it will be a useful tool that can offer assistance and insight to both the novice and experienced grantseeker.

Thanks are due to the many people who contributed directly and indirectly to this workbook. Several deserve special mention. The primary author of this effort was Mim Carlson, a nonprofit management consultant/trainer who works with the Support Center for Nonprofit Management in San Francisco. Mim teaches a popular Support Center proposal writing workshop, and much of the material in the workbook comes from this training program. We are indebted to Mim for agreeing to lead this project. Two other individuals made significant contributions and deserve special thanks for their time and energy: Jan Masaoka, executive director of the Support Center for Nonprofit Management, contributed much to the budgeting section, and Jane Arsenault, executive director of the Support Center of Rhode Island, developed and wrote the section on evaluation. Rick Smith, national executive director of the Support Centers of America, and Rick McCracken, SCA development director, contributed their knowledge of proposal writing and offered regular editorial guidance. Finally, hundreds of nonprofit grantseekers, through participation in Support Center programs, have helped inform us about the multifaceted aspects of grantwriting and the diverse needs of grantseekers. To all of them we owe our special thanks.

And finally, we wish to acknowledge the Grantsmanship Center for its pioneering work in the development of a widely accepted grant proposal framework for nonprofit organizations and grantmakers. Their work has served the sector well for over two decades and remains a strong foundation for the universe of current and future grant writers.

How to Use This Workbook

Winning Grants Step by Step will improve your ability to turn an idea that requires funding into a proposal that merits funding. It is a workbook with a step-by-step approach to successful proposal development, whether for a community nonprofit organization, an educational institution, a hospital, a research facility, or for yourself. Its exercises are designed to help you develop your proposal planning and writing skills and to meet the requirements of both government agencies and private funders.

Winning Grants Step by Step is designed for those with limited experience in preparing proposals, whether they are staff members of nonprofit organizations, people aiming to enter the nonprofit world, or individuals seeking funding for their own creative projects. The process used in the workbook is specific to program/project funding, although it can be easily adapted to general support funding.

The basic idea behind *Winning Grants Step by Step* is that your proposal must reflect a well-planned project and that grant resources given to you should be used wisely. Funders should see that your project is meeting a genuine community need and that it is doing so at a reasonable cost. One of the most common flaws grant-makers find in proposals is lack of clarity about what the group is trying to achieve, the importance of the need, and the plan for meeting it cost-effectively.

Prior to actually writing the proposal, you must have a good idea that is of interest to funders. Step One of this workbook helps you determine what program ideas may be fundable. After the proposal idea is identified and determined to be fundable, a plan should be developed for the idea. For the purposes of this workbook, planning the project will be done as various proposal components are developed.

You will be able to develop your idea into an effective proposal using Steps Two through Seven of the workbook. The Special Resource Section will help you identify interested funders and secure funding by targeting your proposal to meet their priorities. Resource C, for example, provides an opportunity to evaluate a sample proposal through the funder's eyes, giving you an idea of what happens to your proposal once a funder receives it.

The example proposal developed throughout the workbook describes a meals on wheels consortium similar to an existing one. The program is representative of one the real organization may implement. This is an actual group of programs serving meals to frail elders, and the proposal developed has been used successfully for funding.

Certain elements of the workbook have been modified since the original printing. The checklists, for example, are now review questions and some in-text lists have been revised.

The best way to use *Winning Grants Step by Step* is to go through it from beginning to end. The workbook is unique because it is structured to follow the process normally used when preparing a proposal; you can—and should—develop one of your own as you read the book and complete the exercises. Remember, there is no real mystery to successful proposals. They simply take good planning, good writing, good research, and an approach that is geared to your prospective funder.

Introduction

An Overview of the Proposal Writing Process

Grants are a key source of support for many nonprofit organizations, particularly new organizations or those starting new programs. Writing proposals for grants is an inexpensive way to raise funds, because the writing and research do not cost much money (just lots of your time!). A strong proposal—that is, a well-written, well-organized proposal—can bring in substantial income for your organization.

A well-prepared proposal can also build an organization's credibility with funders. Organizations that have the respect of funders are often called upon to work on particular issues of concern to both you and your funder. This gives you an opportunity to help make community changes on a larger scale than your organization may be capable of accomplishing alone.

Although proposal writing is a popular and effective way to fund programs, you should understand that it is only one way to increase revenues. There are several different techniques used to raise funds, and it is important to use the right technique at the right time for the right purpose in order to be successful.

Most funds raised in the private sector come from individuals. As shown in Table 1, $126.2 billion was raised in 1993; approximately 88 percent came from individuals, either in the form of direct gifts or bequests.

In addition to private sources of funds, government funding adds billions of grant dollars that are available to nonprofits. Government funds may come directly from a federal agency, such as Health and Human Services, or through a state or local government agency. Funds from the government are usually targeted for very specific purposes, so having a good idea is especially important for this funding source.

TABLE I.1. Revenue from Private Sources: 1993 Figures.		
SOURCES	**AMOUNT IN BILLIONS**	**PERCENT OF TOTAL**
Individuals	$102.5	81.2 percent
Bequests	$8.5	6.8 percent
Foundations	$9.2	7.3 percent
Corporations	$5.9	4.7 percent
TOTAL	$126.2	100.0 percent

Note: Totals and percentage changes incorporate computer rounding.
Source: Data reprinted from p. 10 of *Giving USA,* 1994, a publication of the AAFRC—Trust for Philanthropy (New York), by permission.

HELPFUL HINT

Relying on just one funding source may be detrimental to one's fundraising efforts. The old adage of not putting all your eggs in one basket certainly applies to raising sufficient funds. Organizations with a fundraising program using several different techniques (direct mail solicitations, grantwriting, and special events, to name a few) are generally the most successful in the long run.

■ Categories of Support

One reason an organization needs to use several different fundraising techniques is that there are generally several areas of financial need in an organization. Usually, an organization seeks support in one or more of the following categories:

1. *Operating (general support):* Funds for operations are used to cover the costs of running programs to meet community needs. The funds come from earned income, corporate or foundation grants, interest from an endowment, direct mail campaigns and special events, and such ongoing efforts as an annual fund.

2. *Special projects:* Funds for special projects are monies restricted by the funder to starting a new program or undertaking a project with a limited time frame. Foundations, corporations, some individuals, and government agencies are interested in supporting special projects.

3. *Capital/equipment:* Funds for capital support are raised through a capital campaign, which is an intensive effort to generate a specified amount of funds for construction, remodeling and renovation, building expansion, and the purchase of land or equipment. Methods used for capital campaigns are individual major gift solicitation and proposal writing to corporations and foundations. Some government agencies also have funds for capital projects.

4. *Endowments:* Funds for endowments are sometimes generated through planned gifts, which are given by an individual to an organization as part of a will or trust. They may also be received as part of a capital/endowment campaign utilizing the methods for raising capital/equipment funds. Generally the principal of the endowment is held as a long-term investment for the organization while the income is used each year for operating needs.

■ The Proposal Process

There is no mystery to writing a successful proposal. The keys to success are

Developing a clear program plan
Researching funders thoroughly
Targeting your proposals carefully
Writing a concise proposal

Proposals generally follow a widely accepted format, although funders may change the format to fit their needs. Whether the fundseeker is preparing a proposal for a foundation, a corporation, or a government funder, the process of proposal development will be essentially the same. It traditionally begins with development of a program plan and ends with the necessary steps to follow up with funders after your proposal has been submitted. This book covers the process in detail in Steps One through Eleven. The major components of a proposal are as follows:

Cover letter: Accompanies the proposal and briefly describes its significance.

Summary: A very brief (usually one-page) overview of the proposal

Introduction: Presents the organization's qualifications to carry out the proposed program plan

Need statement: A compelling description of the need to be addressed by the applicant organization

Objectives: Spells out what specific results or outcomes are to be accomplished

Methods: Describes the programs and services to achieve the desired results

Evaluation: Describes a plan for assessing program accomplishments

Future funding: Provides an agency's strategies for developing additional funding to continue the program after initial grant funding is over

Budget: A line-item summary of program revenues and expenses

The format given in this book is generally what is used for all funders, including many government sources. It is an orderly way to develop your thoughts and to present your project. Bear in mind that there are funders—particularly government funders—who have certain formats that they expect you to follow when preparing a proposal. It is always important to follow their specific instructions.

■ Types of Proposals

A *letter of intent* is a two-page summary mailed when the funder wishes to see a brief description of the project before making a decision on whether to ask for a longer, more detailed proposal. A letter of intent must focus on how the proposed project fits the priorities of the funder.

A *letter proposal* is the type most often requested by corporations. It is a three-page description of the project plan, the organization requesting the funds, and the actual request.

The *long-proposal format,* including the cover letter and proposal summary, is the type most often requested by foundation and government funders. Corporations should not receive this format unless they specifically request it. The writer has an opportunity in the longer proposal to give many details about the project and its importance to the community. In this longer format you should make sure the funding request is not hidden. It should appear both in the cover letter and in the summary.

■ Tips for Writing Proposals

Take the approach of having one writer and a review team of several people. Everyone has a different writing style, and too many writers might make the proposal read poorly. The person writing the proposal, obviously, must have excellent writing skills. However, the writer may also be one of the individuals participating in the planning phase of the project; the proposal will suffer if the writer does not have an understanding of what the project is, why it is important to the community, and why the organization seeking funding is the best qualified to undertake the project.

The following principles should be adhered to when preparing the proposal:

- *First and foremost, a good proposal should flow and build from one component section to the next.* A proposal is really nothing more than a business plan for implementing a nonprofit program. The proposal components discussed above outline the body of the plan. Together, the components of a proposal make a case for the need to do something about a community need.

- *Use a positive writing style, but present a well-reasoned, thoughtful presentation.* A grant proposal is not an emotional appeal. Typically readers are professional grantmakers. They need to understand the cause and effect of your case. Whenever possible, explain assumptions and present evidence that supports major assertions about the scope of a problem or the efficacy of a particular method.

- *Avoid jargon and don't overwrite.* Make it easy for someone who probably is not an expert in your particular field to read your entire proposal. Jargon (words that only people in a specialized field will understand) acts as a barrier to understanding, and people cannot be sympathetic to things they cannot comprehend. Also remember that grantmakers have to do a lot of reading; you will be doing yourself and them a favor by keeping your proposal brief and focused on the main points. Be thrifty with your words, but don't sacrifice important points to achieve brevity.

- *Don't use a shotgun approach with your proposal.* After you have a developed a proposal, tailor it to the specific instructions of each funder. While it is true that most grantmakers want the same basic information, it is also true that they request it in different formats. This will mean reordering sections, cutting and pasting, and possibly relabeling some sections (for instance, *the needs statement* may become *the problem statement*). Occasionally, you will have to add or subtract material from the original version. By tailoring your proposal for each grantmaker, you will be giving each proposal reviewer confidence that the proposal is responding to the funder's concerns.

- *Get some honest feedback on your proposal before you send it to a funder.* Ask one or two people (maybe a staff or board member or even someone outside your organization) to critically review the proposal. Did everything make sense? Was the need clear? Did the proposed methods and objectives seem like an appropriate response to the need? Use their feedback to strengthen the final proposal.

- *Make the proposal visually attractive, but don't overdo it.* Whenever possible, break up the written page. Use reasonable margins and use bulleted lists and other formatting tools to make each page a little more inviting.

Developing the Proposal Idea

Now that you have had an introduction to the process of preparing a proposal, it's time to take the first step. In this section of the workbook you will develop your proposal idea by answering some key questions.

■ Identifying Fundable Projects and Programs

Before actually writing a proposal, you should determine which projects in your organization are most likely to be funded through a grant. Most funders prefer to give grants in support of special projects and new ideas rather than general operating expenses of an organization or the ongoing costs of established programs. Special projects may include new programs or expansion of current programs in new directions.

Generally, organizations should plan new projects using a team approach involving staff, clients, and volunteers. The planning team develops a project plan first and then uses it when writing the components of the proposal. Since most grants mean a change will take place in the organization, it is important to involve people in the organization with the planning because they will be more enthusiastic about implementing the change and the design of the project will be better.

To help in developing a fundable proposal idea, answer the six questions in Worksheet 1.1. After answering the questions in the worksheet, you and your organization should choose an idea that you would like to develop using the exercises that are in this book. By the time you are finished with the workbook, you will have a fully developed proposal to mail to funders you have researched.

When preparing a proposal, writers will generally start with the planning sections (need statement, objectives, methods, evaluation, future funding, and budget). Then they will write the introduction section, finishing with the summary and cover letter. This workbook follows that format.

The planning sections of the proposal are written first because they deserve careful attention; without a clearly articulated project plan, it is very difficult to get funding. Generally, organizations will spend approximately 80 percent of their time planning a project and only 20 percent writing and packaging the proposal.

The following several steps will help you define your answers to these questions while creating your own well-planned proposal. Examples and worksheets are in the workbook to assist you in the process.

WORKSHEET 1.1.	Proposal Idea Questionnaire.

1. What new projects (or program expansions) are you planning for the next two to three years?

    Project A:

    Project B:

    Project C:

    Project D:

2. Which of the above projects are compatible with your current mission and purpose? (For those projects outside of your mission, considerable justification will be necessary to convince a funder to support the project.)

Project	Compatible with mission	Not compatible (Check whichever applies)
A		
B		
C		
D		

3. Who else is doing these projects? Is there duplication of effort? Can a partnership be formed that will benefit all organizations concerned with a project?

Project	Duplicate project	Possible collaboration (Check if applicable)
A		
B		
C		
D		

4. What community need does each of your projects address?

Project	Need addressed
A	
B	
C	
D	

5. What members of your community—including civic leaders, political figures, the media, and your own clients—support each project?

Project	Supporters
A	
B	
C	
D	

6. Does your organization currently have the expertise to undertake each project? Will new staff be necessary? Can the organization manage growth in personnel effectively?

HELPFUL HINT

To develop a project idea into a plan, you need to answer the following six questions:

- What is the community need that the plan is addressing?
  Answering this question develops the *need statement* component of a proposal.

- What would an improved community situation look like?
  Answering this question develops the *objectives* component of a proposal.

- What can this organization do to improve the situation?
  Answering this question develops the *methods* component of a proposal.

- How will it be determined that the project has succeeded?
  Answering this question develops the *evaluation* component of a proposal.

- How much will the project cost?
  Answering this question develops the *budget* component of a proposal.

- How will the project be funded in the future?
  Answering this question develops the *future funding* component of a proposal.

Writing a Compelling Need Statement

In this step, you will learn the key elements of a need statement, including the four requirements of a successful statement. Then, through exercises, you will prepare a statement of need for your own proposal.

■ Preparing Your Need Statement

The place to begin writing a proposal is the statement of need. A need statement describes a critical condition or set of conditions or a social need affecting certain people or things in a specific place at a specific time. This component of your proposal answers the question, What is the community need to be addressed?

Preparing the statement of need is a critical part of the proposal, since funders must agree with the organization that the project meets an important need. It is often the compelling need statement that motivates a funder to help.

The need statement is at the heart of your entire case for support. If the reader does not understand and agree with your presentation of the need (or problem), he or she will not have any reason to pay much attention to the rest of your proposal. As one veteran grantwriter once said, "problems sell!" In other words, your need statement is the proverbial hook. There are several major points to keep in mind when developing your need statement. First, the need to be addressed in your proposal should have some clear relationship to your organization's mission and purpose. Second, your need statement should not emphasize organizational needs but rather focus on a need in the community. Third, any assertions about the need should be well supported with evidence (for example, statistical facts, expert testimony, and so on). Fourth, the need that is described in the proposal should be consistent with the scope of your organization's ability to respond to that need (which will be described in subsequent sections of the proposal). Finally, make the need statement easy to read by eliminating any jargon that might act as a communication barrier.

The need your organization is addressing can be very specific to your geographic area, or it can be one that is found in many communities. If the need occurs in an area larger than that served by your organization, it is important to focus only on what you can reasonably accomplish with your program. However, the work you do can become a model for other organizations in other locations. By taking a "model approach," the organization broadens the base of potential funders to include those who may be concerned with the need in other areas.

If you want your program to be a model for others, you would mention in this section that your organization is addressing the need on a larger level through development of a model program. In the methods component (discussed in Step Four) you would discuss how the information would be disseminated to other organizations.

■ Tips for Writing the Need Statement

- State the need using hard-core statistics, not assumptions or undocumented assertions parading as facts.
- Use statistics that are clear and that support your argument.
- Use comparative statistics and research, when possible.
- Make sure all data collection is well documented.
- Use touching stories of people as examples.
- Focus your explanation of the need on the geographic area you can serve.

Worksheet 2.1 lists a series of questions for you to answer to help you clearly define the need you are addressing. It is accompanied by a sample "completed" questionnaire. Following the worksheet is a Sample Need Statement. After completing the questionnaire and reading the sample statement of need, write your own statement of need based on the information you have developed. Then, using the Need Statement Review Questions at the end of this section, make sure you have written your statement well. Rewrite your need statement until you feel you have addressed all the questions.

■ Sample Need Statement

Twenty percent of the population of ABC County are seniors sixty-five and older. The fastest growing sector of this demographic group is the frail elderly population described as persons eighty-five and older. The Department on Aging recently conducted a survey among frail elders to find out what they needed most to stay in their homes. Their highest priority according to the survey was information about services to seniors in the county and assistance in accessing them.

Within this county there is a growing number of social services available for the rapidly expanding population of elderly individuals. Seniors can have errands run for them through an errand service, obtain door-to-door transportation to doctors' appointments, receive a daily checkup phone call, obtain legal or financial-planning assistance, and have someone make safety repairs on their homes.

Unfortunately, as services for seniors are flourishing, a homebound person's ability to access these services is diminishing because of the loss of county funding for social workers. There has been a 25 percent reduction in social workers in this county in the past two years. Each remaining social worker has a minimum caseload of 150 individuals, which makes regular home visits virtually impossible. Additionally, there are no longer any social workers who specialize in gerontology; the workers who are active have limited effectiveness with the homebound elderly.

None of the frail older adults served by the Meals Consortium members have regular social workers to help them with services that will allow them to stay in their homes. The result is that an older person's daily nutrition needs are being met by our programs, but equally important social service needs are not. Without a coordinated system that serves the health and social service needs of this population, an elderly person's risk of being institutionalized is high.

As an example, Mrs. X has been receiving Meals on Wheels for three years. She is eighty-two years old and is unable to walk for more than a few steps due to severe arthritis. She has other medical problems as well. Her family lives in another state and visits only during the holidays. Mrs. X receives her daily meal from Meals on Wheels, but she relies on the good will of her neighbors to pick up some groceries for her and take her to the doctor. The neighbors are not always available to help her, and Mrs. X has missed important appointments and gone hungry because she is homebound.

WORKSHEET 2.1.   Statement of Need Questionnaire.

Use the filled-out example on the next page to help you complete this questionnaire.

WHO? WHERE? WHEN?	WHAT? WHY?	EVIDENCE OF PROBLEM	SO WHAT?
Who are the people with the need?	What is the need?	What evidence do you have to support your claim?	What are the consequences of meeting the need?
Where are the people?			
When is the need evident?			
	Why does this need occur?		How is the need linked to your organization?

WORKSHEET 2.1. Statement of Need Questionnaire.

Use this filled-out example to help you complete the questionnaire on the preceding page.

WHO? WHERE? WHEN?	WHAT? WHY?	EVIDENCE OF PROBLEM	SO WHAT?
Who are the people with the need?	What is the need?	What evidence do you have to support your claim?	What are the consequences of meeting the need?
Frail homebound seniors over sixty years old, living at home, usually alone	■ *No comprehensive assessment relating nutritional and social service needs happens on a regular basis for homebound elders.* ■ *The lack of need identification and referral for services results in deteriorating health for the person and frequently results in costly institutionalization that could be prevented.*	■ *More than 13,000 individuals in the county over age sixty live below the poverty line.* ■ *Social workers are not available to visit the homebound elderly.* ■ *Many Meals on Wheels recipients must leave their homes because of the lack of coordinated care.*	■ *Frail elders will be able to remain in their home longer.* ■ *Frail elders will remain healthier with good coordination between social services and nutrition programs.* ■ *Expensive institutionalization will be avoided through cost-effective preventive services.*
Where are the people?			
Throughout ABC County			
When is the need evident?			
When illness or institutionalization occurs due to an absence of social services	Why does this need occur?		How is the need linked to your organization?
	■ *No organization has social workers working with nutritionists to assess the health and social services needs of the homebound elderly.* ■ *Funding is not available at each organization to hire social workers.*		*The Meals Consortium mission is to find cost-effective ways to serve the county's frail elders. The social services program will provide a coordinated system of social services and nutritional care to serve the target population.*

Mrs. X was not aware of the errand program or transportation service for homebound older adults until a Meals on Wheels volunteer mentioned them to her. If social workers had been available to assess Mrs. X's needs and make referrals, she would have more quickly received the help she requires.

This example is representative of the difficulties faced by many homebound individuals and of the frustrations faced by staff who want to help frail elders stay in their homes. Social workers available to focus on the needs of this population with appropriate referrals and follow-up would make a valuable difference in the quality of life of all persons served.

The solution of coordinating nutrition and social services for the homebound elderly is crucial. A recent report from the county's Department on Aging indicated that intervention with comprehensive dietary and social services will prolong an older person's ability to stay at home, thus giving them the independence they seek and helping to hold down the high costs of institutionalization.

The member organizations of the Meals Consortium have been providing quality nutrition services to frail older individuals for many years. No other organization in the county provides direct services to this special population, making the Meals Consortium the most likely nonprofit to fill this important gap in services. The addition of a social services referral program, coordinated by the Consortium, is seen as a cost-effective way to provide more comprehensive care to the homebound.

■ Need Statement Review Questions

Have you discussed the need in terms of your project's or program's benefit to the individuals in the community who will be its customers (and not to your organization)?

Does the described need have a clear relationship to your organization's mission and goals?

Given your organization's size and resources, can you meet the need in a meaningful way?

Does your statement include solid evidence supporting your claims about the nature, size, and scope of the need to be addressed?

Have you eliminated jargon and acronyms from the narrative?

Is your need statement persuasive without being overly wordy?

Defining Clear Goals and Objectives

In this section, you will learn how to write clear goals and objectives. A distinction is made between *outcome* and *process* objectives, so that you will understand the important differences between the two. An outcome objective states a quantifiable result of the project. A process objective quantifies your method. Using the worksheets and following the examples, you will write a set of objectives for your own proposal.

■ Writing Goals and Objectives

Once the need to be met has been agreed upon and written into a need statement, it is necessary to develop goals and objectives to give a clear picture of the results of implementing your program. The goals and objectives are the outcomes of the planned program, and they answer the question, How would the situation look if it were changed?

■ Definition

A *goal* is a broad-based statement of the ultimate result of the change being undertaken (a result that is sometimes unreachable in the short term).

Example: The homebound elderly in ABC County will live with dignity and independence in their own homes.

Program goals are often written for the organization as part of a long-range planning process. They may already be developed for you. A funder will want to know what your program goals are, so they should be included in this section of the proposal.

■ Definition

An *objective* is a measurable, time-specific result that the organization expects to accomplish as part of the grant. It is much more narrowly defined than a goal. Like the goal, the objective is tied to the need statement.

Example: There will be a 5 percent decrease in the number of frail older adults going into convalescent homes during the first year of the social services referral program.

Preparing the objectives component of the proposal should be done while keeping the following in mind:

- Objectives should be stated in quantifiable terms.
- Objectives should be stated in terms of outcomes, not methods and inputs; that is, they should specify the result of an activity as opposed to just describing program methods.
- Objectives should clearly identify the population group being served.
- Objectives should be realistic and capable of being accomplished within the time frame indicated.

Program objectives should be written as the outcome of your methods, not as the methods themselves. If you look at this from an ends-and-means perspective, the objectives are the ends, and the methods are the means of reaching those ends. The example above is an *outcome objective*—that is, it describes a result. The methods (discussed in Step Four) indicate what will be done to start the new program, increase social services referrals, and lead to the accomplishment of the objective.

When developing each objective, answering the following five questions helps to clearly articulate the result you expect to accomplish:

1. What is/are the key area(s) you are seeking to change?
2. What segment of the population will be involved in the change?
3. What is the direction of change (increase or improvement, or decrease or reduction) you'll be looking for?
4. What is the degree or amount of change you'll be looking for?
5. What is the deadline to reach the degree of change?

HELPFUL HINT

One easy way to ensure you are writing a good objective is to start your objective with wordings, such as the following, that suggest a purpose:
  To reduce ...
  To increase ...
  To decrease ...
  To expand ...

■ Tips for Writing Good Goals and Objectives

- Goals and objectives should tie directly to the need statement.
- Include all relevant parties in the target population.
- Allow plenty of time for the objectives to be accomplished; things always take longer than planned.
- Objectives do not describe methods. Opening a new spay/neuter clinic is a method. Reducing pet overpopulation by 10 percent in 1993 is an objective, because it describes a result.
- Determine how you are going to measure the change you are projecting in your objective. If you find you have no way to measure change, you probably need to rethink the objective (more on this in Step Five).

Develop your objectives using Worksheet 3.1. Then write your goals and objectives component using the Sample Goals and Objectives as a guide. When you are finished,

WORKSHEET 3.1. **Goals and Objectives Exercise.**

Write your objectives by using the following worksheet to help you focus on outcomes. Start by indicating the goal of the program, and then describe the objectives that tie to the goal. You may have more than one goal (use separate sheets for each goal). You should limit your objectives to one to four per goal.

GOAL: _____

	OBJECTIVE ONE	OBJECTIVE TWO	OBJECTIVE THREE	OBJECTIVE FOUR
Area of change				
Target population				
Direction of change				
Time frame				
Degree of change				

Standard Form for Objective Statements: to (direction of change) + (area of change) + (target population) + (degree of change) + (time frame).

WORKSHEET 3.1. **Goals and Objectives Exercise.**

Use this filled-out example to help you complete the exercise on the preceding page.

GOAL: *Increase the quality of life for the elderly at risk of institutionalization.*

	OBJECTIVE ONE	**OBJECTIVE TWO**	**OBJECTIVE THREE**	**OBJECTIVE FOUR**
Area of change	*Individuals leaving the Consortium for institutions*	*Individuals remaining in their homes*	*Social services referrals and follow-up services*	*Social services direct care*
Target population	*Persons served by the Meals Consortium who are at risk of institutionali-zation*	*Individuals served by the Meals Consortium*	*Individuals served by the Meals Consortium*	*Individuals who are most vulnerable served by the Meals Consortium*
Direction of change	*Reduce*	*Expand*	*Increase*	*Increase*
Time frame	*12 months*	*12 months*	*12 months*	*12 months*
Degree of change	*5%*	*80%*	*75%*	*90%*

Standard Form for Objective Statements: to (direction of change) + (area of change) + (target population) + (degree of change) + (time frame).

go through the Goals and Objectives Review Questions in the same way you did for your statement of need. Remember, you want to answer yes to each question in the Goals and Objectives Review Questions.

■ Sample Goals and Objectives

The primary goal of the Meal Consortium is to enable homebound frail elders to live with independence and dignity in their own homes. Without the daily nutritional meals, the homebound would risk malnourishment and deteriorating health since they are unable to prepare their own meals. The alternative for most of the individuals served is costly institutionalization. A secondary goal of the Meal Consortium is to prevent the cost burden of institutionalization for the homebound and for the community.

The project being proposed will help meet the Consortium's goals. The following objectives are specific to the proposed social services referral program.

OUTCOME OBJECTIVES

1. Reduce by 5 percent the number of individuals leaving the Meals Consortium to be institutionalized due to lack of social services.
2. Expand care of the frail elderly to ensure that 80 percent of the population served by the Meals Consortium remain in their homes during 1994–95.

PROCESS OBJECTIVES

1. Increase social services referrals and follow-up for 75 percent of the individuals served by the Meals Consortium during 1994–95.
2. Increase social services direct care to 90 percent of the most vulnerable homebound elders served by the Meals Consortium.

■ Goals and Objectives Review Questions

Are your goals stated as results?

Are your objectives stated as specific results that relate to a program goal?

Can progress in meeting your objectives be quantified and assessed?

Do your objectives describe the client population and a specific time frame for change?

Developing Your Methods

In this section you will determine the methods you will use to reach your objectives. You will look at the elements of the methods component of a proposal and will see how a timeline can be used to help you and prospective funders outline what will happen when. Using the worksheets and following examples, you will write your methods for the objectives you developed in Step Three.

■ Writing the Methods Component

When the goals and objectives for the project being undertaken have been determined, it is time to plan how you will achieve those results. The methods component of the proposal tells funders how an organization will accomplish the objectives and answers the question, What can the organization do to change the situation?

A method is a detailed description of the activities to be implemented to achieve the ends specified in the objectives. Methods are also frequently referred to as activities or strategies. Regardless of what you call them, this section of the proposal should clearly describe the methods to be used and give good reasons for why these methods were chosen. The section should include a description of program staffing along with an identification of the client populations to be served and justification of why they were selected.

To develop the methods component, answer the following questions:

- What are the "givens" that are inflexible, such as date of completion, dollars available, staff available?
- What activities need to be done in order to meet the objective?
- What are the starting and ending dates of the activities?
- Who has responsibility for completing each activity?
- How will participants be selected? (This question is not applicable to some projects.)
- How was this methodology determined to be the correct one to solve the problem presented? Does this build on models already in existence, or is this a different approach? Why is it superior?

The methods section should be reasonable in that activities should be able to be accomplished within the time frame of the proposal and with the resources available. For proposals with numerous objectives and methods, it is a good idea to include a timeline showing when methods will start and finish. The following is an example of one way to chart your activities on a timeline:

EXAMPLE OF TIMELINE

ACTIVITY	MONTH	1	2	3	4	5	6	7	8	9	10	11	12
1. Hire a program coordinator.		___											
2. Recruit two social workers.			___										
3. Identify elders with priority needs to be addressed.				___									
4. Begin implementation with persons needing immediate assistance.					_____ (ongoing)								
5. Purchase equipment and materials for office.				_____									
6. Hire social services support staff.					_____								
7. Develop individual service plans to meet needs of each homebound person.						_____							
8. Fully implement social services program.								_____ (ongoing)					

■   **Tips for Writing the Methods Component**

- Tie the methods to your objectives and to your need statement.
- Ensure that methods are congruent with resources requested in the budget.
- Explain the rationale for choosing your methods; talk in terms of research findings, expert opinion, and your own past experience with similar programs.
- State what facilities and capital equipment will be available for the project.
- Build various phases of activities on one another to move effort toward the desired results. Include a timeline.
- Be sure to discuss who will be served and how they will be chosen.
- Don't assume the reviewer knows more than he/she does about the project.

Develop your methods by completing Worksheet 4.1. Then use the Sample Methods Component to write your own methods section for your proposal. Use the Methods Review Questions to review your methods, just as you did for the need statement and your goals and objectives.

HELPFUL HINT

The length of the methods section of a proposal varies depending on the size of the project being undertaken. A general rule is to give the funder a clear picture of all the important steps you will take to accomplish each objective you have indicated in your goals and objectives section. Government proposals often expect considerably more information than other funders for this part of the proposal.

WORKSHEET 4.1. Methods Exercise.

List the key elements of your planned program. Use the filled-out chart on the next page as an example. Then write a methods section for your proposal.

TASKS/SUBTASKS	RESOURCES NEEDED	START AND FINISH DATES

WORKSHEET 4.1. Methods Exercise.

Use this filled-out example to help you complete the chart on the preceding page.

TASKS/SUBTASKS	RESOURCES NEEDED	START AND FINISH DATES
Hire a program coordinator	*Funds for salary, benefits; pool of candidates; job descriptions*	*First six weeks of program*
Program coordinator hires two social workers	*Funds for salaries, benefits; pool of candidates; job descriptions*	*Within three months of program's start-up*
Set up offices and obtain equipment and supplies	*Funds for equipment, supplies; in-kind donations; list of supplies and equipment needed*	*Within three months of program's start-up*
Identify those elders with priority social services referral needs and begin referrals	*Consortium members' assessments of Meals on Wheels recipients; establishment of priorities*	*Within three months of program*
Hire necessary support staff	*Plan for support staff needed; funds for support staff; pool of applicants; job descriptions*	*First four months of program*
Implement the program plan	*Staff in place with understanding of plan*	*Sixth month of program and after*

■ **Sample Methods Component**

To accomplish the objectives stated in the previous section, the Meals Consortium will use the following methods. It was decided to follow this course of action because of the success of model social services and nutrition programs that were developed using these same strategies. A timeline is in the appendices; it gives expected starting/ending dates for each activity.

OBJECTIVE ONE:

Increase social services referrals and follow-up for 75 percent of the individuals served by the Meals Consortium.

METHODS:

- Consortium members will hire a social services program coordinator within the first two months of the program.
- The program coordinator will hire two additional social workers within the first four months of the program.
- Consortium members will ensure that office equipment and supplies are available for the coordinator, social workers, and support staff within the first four months of the program.
- The program coordinator and social workers will work with Consortium members to identify those most in need of social services and begin referrals and follow-up within the first three months of the program.
- The program coordinator will hire any support staff within the first six months of the program.
- The program coordinator and social workers will fully implement the plan beginning in the sixth month of the new program.

(The other two objectives from the goals and objectives section would be identified with methods using the same format as in this sample.)

■ **Methods Review Questions**

Do the methods discussed in the proposal derive logically from the need statement and the goals and objectives?

Do your methods present the program activities to be undertaken?

Have you explained why you selected specific methods or activities?

Have you explained the timing and order of specific activities?

Is it clear who will perform specific activities?

Given projected resources, are the proposed activities feasible?

Preparing the Evaluation Component

After the methods are determined it is important to plan how your program will be evaluated. In this section of the workbook you will learn how to write an evaluation plan, so that you can effectively demonstrate that your program was successful. The exercises will help you think about what your evaluation plan should contain.

■ Planning the Evaluation Component

An evaluation is a process that determines the effectiveness and efficiency of a project. Decisions made during this process help an organization plan for the project's future and reassure funders that their financial commitment is being well spent.

How a program will be evaluated must be determined prior to the program's implementation. Bear in mind that funders expect to know the ways an organization will measure the success of a project.

There is much that can be gained from putting thought and effort into an effective evaluation design.

The first benefit is that we strengthen the proposal in the eye of the reviewers. Each time we ask a funder to invest in our programs, we ask them to place a bet with us that the world as we see it will be improved in some specific way because of our efforts. Essentially, each time we devise a program, we are testing a hypothesis ("If we do this . . . then that will happen"). A solid evaluation component can help to reassure a funder that we are interested, as they are, in learning whether our hypothesis is correct.

The second benefit that accrues to the organization is that we learn what is going well and what is not. The process of thinking through an evaluation design can strengthen programs before they are implemented. The knowledge gained through an evaluation can be shared within the organization to improve programs as they are implemented. This knowledge can also be shared with the outside world to allow others to learn from our work.

The third benefit is to the public. Every time we ask for and receive funding we are the recipients of public trust. We have an obligation to ensure that our program is having the effect we intended. Evaluation is one of the strongest tools we have to make sure we are meeting this obligation.

Figuring out how to evaluate the program you have proposed is a thinking exercise. Behind every program is a "theory of action"—a set of beliefs, held by those who oversee the program, about how the means lead to the ends. Determining the relationship between your expected outcomes and the program efforts and explaining what is important to evaluate and why are the first steps in preparing your evaluation component.

To develop your theory of action, you should think of the following five elements, which all programs contain:

- *Inputs:* All those resources that are assembled before the program begins, such as clients, staff, materials, facilities, and equipment
- *Throughputs:* The methods of the program that employ the resources
- *Outputs:* The immediate results for the client that are the effects of the throughput process
- *Outcomes:* The effects of the program on the client's life or the societal need addressed
- *Impacts:* The longer-term benefits to the client and/or society

Here are the elements as applied to the Meals on Wheels Consortium:

- *Inputs:* Program staff, seniors served by the programs, office space, supplies, equipment
- *Throughputs:* All the methods described in the methods section of this workbook
- *Outputs:* The number of seniors receiving referrals for social services
- *Outcomes:* Increased number of seniors staying longer in their homes
- *Impacts:* Increased quality of life for seniors, reduced medical costs for caring for frail elders in nursing homes

Determine the elements of your own program by answering the questions in Worksheet 5.1.

Organizations conduct evaluations in order to do five things:

- Find out whether the program did what was expected
- Determine if the methods specified were used and the objectives met
- Determine if an impact was made on the need identified
- Obtain feedback from their target group and others
- Maintain some control over the project
- Make adjustments during the program to help its success

When preparing the evaluation section of your proposal, ask yourself the following questions to help frame what you will say:

- What is the purpose of your evaluation?
- How will the findings be used?
- What will you know after the evaluation that you do not know now?
- What will you do after the evaluation that you cannot do now for lack of information?
- How will you know if you have succeeded with your program?

It is not possible within the framework of this workbook to provide detailed information on program evaluation methods. However, a brief overview should help you determine the methods that are most appropriate for the evaluation you conduct.

There are two approaches you can take to collecting your data. You can use quantitative methods, or you can use qualitative.

Quantitative methods translate experience into units that can be counted, compared, measured, and manipulated statistically. Data analysis techniques include

WORKSHEET 5.1. Identify Your Program Elements.

1. What are the inputs for your program?

2. What are the throughputs? (You may have answered this question with your proposal methods from the previous exercise.)

3. What are the outputs of your program?

4. What are the outcomes?

5. What are the impacts?

descriptive statistics (averages, means, percentiles, and frequency distribution) as well as inferential statistics (sign tests, simple linear regression, and chi-square). These allow us to make statements about cause-and-effect relationships.

Quantitative methods are most appropriate if your questions involve

- Understanding the quantities or frequency of particular aspects of a program (for example, number of enrollees, number of dropouts)
- Determining if a cause-and-effect relationship does occur
- Comparing two different methods that are seeking to achieve the same outcomes
- Establishing numerical baselines; pretests, posttests, and six-month or one-year follow-up

Qualitative methods are rooted in direct contact with the people involved in a program and consist of three kinds of data collection: interviews (group and/or individual), direct or field observation, and review of certain documents.

Qualitative methods are most appropriate if your questions involve

- Understanding participants' or staff or community feelings or opinions about a program
- Gaining insight into how the patterns of relationships within the program unfold
- Gathering multiple perspectives to understand the whole
- Identifying approximate indicators that clients are moving in the right direction

Both qualitative and quantitative methods have value. The most important thing to remember is to find the right fit between the method you choose, the questions you want answered, and the information needs of those asking the question. Often, a mix of both quantitative and qualitative methods yields the best results.

An example of using a methodological mix of collecting both quantitative and qualitative data would be conducting a pretest and a posttest in a classroom to determine changes in the knowledge of students (quantitative). In addition, evaluators would passively observe the class and the facility in which the curriculum is taught to better understand the students' experience (qualitative).

The evaluation component of the proposal should include a brief summary of the data collection methods being used for the project. The evaluation component must tie to the objectives and methods previously described in the proposal. If objectives are measurable and methods time-specific, it will be easier to prepare a good data collection plan and to write a strong evaluation component for the proposal.

Answer the questions in Worksheet 5.2 to begin planning your proposal's evaluation section. An example of a completed exercise is provided to help you get started. Afterward, refer to the Sample Evaluation before writing your own. When you finish writing your evaluation section, review it with the Evaluation Review Questions provided for you.

WORKSHEET 5.2. Evaluation Planning Questions.

Answer the following questions to plan your evaluation.

1. What questions will your evaluation activities seek to answer?

2. What are the specific evaluation plans and time frames?

   What kinds of data will be collected?

   At what points?

   Using what strategies or instruments?

   Using what comparison group or baseline, if any?

3. If you intend to use your study on a sample of participants, how will this sample be constructed?

4. What procedures will you use to determine whether the program was implemented as planned?

5. Who will conduct the evaluation?

6. Who will receive the reports?

WORKSHEET 5.2. Evaluation Planning Questions.

Use this filled-out example to help you answer the questions on the preceding page.

1. What questions will your evaluation activities seek to answer?

   Are the objectives of the program being met?

   Is the program meeting seniors' needs in a cost-effective way?

2. What are the specific evaluation plans and time frames?

   What kinds of data will be collected?

   The number of people leaving a Meals on Wheels program and where they went

   The number of referrals made to each senior and the type of referral; increase in satisfaction of seniors living at home

   At what points?

   Daily for quantitative data; quarterly for qualitative data

   Using what strategies or instruments?

   Computer database tracking system; interviews

   Using what comparison group or baseline, if any?

   Last year's population of persons served

3. If you intend to use your study on a sample of participants, how will this sample be constructed?

   N/A

4. What procedures will you use to determine whether the program was implemented as planned?

   A quarterly review of the methods outlined in the proposal, to determine if they are being carried out in a timely manner

5. Who will conduct the evaluation?

   Program director

6. Who will receive the reports?

   Funders, board members, executive director, other interested individuals and agencies

■ **Sample Evaluation**

At every four-month interval, the program coordinator will measure the new social services referral program's progress toward meeting the three objectives identified in the goals and objectives section of this proposal. Data on each of the individuals needing social services referrals will be collected daily by the social workers and support staff. This data will indicate what referral was made, the reason for the referral, and what a one-week follow-up phone call after the referral indicated. Individuals at greatest risk for institutionalization will receive additional follow-up calls and personal visits by the social workers to ensure that the services needed are being provided. The number of individuals leaving a Meals on Wheels program will be tracked monthly to show how many were institutionalized and why. Each funder of the social services referral program will receive quarterly reports during the first year of the project, as will board members, the executive director, and other interested individuals.

■ **Evaluation Review Questions**

Does the evaluation section focus on assessing the projected results?

Does your evaluation assess the efficiency of program methods?

Does the evaluation describe who will be evaluated and/or what will be measured?

Does your evaluation section state what information will be collected in the evaluation process?

Does the evaluation state who will be responsible for making the assessments?

Does the evaluation section discuss how the information and conclusions will be used to improve the program?

Developing Future Funding Strategies

In this section you will learn ways to find future funding after the initial funders of your program have stopped giving you money. There are many resources available to you to keep your program running, and you will identify, through exercises and examples, the sources of ongoing support that are best for you.

■ Writing the Future Funding Component

Generally, in program planning, future funding is not decided until after the budget is determined for the current program. In proposal writing, however, this section appears as part of the narrative and comes before the budget. For the purposes of this workbook, future funding will be discussed now.

While this is the last narrative section of the proposal it is definitely not the least important. If the project being planned is expected to continue beyond the years of the initial grant, planning needs to be done to determine how the project will be funded.

The content of this section will depend on whether it is part of a program proposal or a capital/equipment proposal.

In a *program proposal*—that is, a proposal describing a new program or the continuation of an existing one—there are two main reasons for having a future funding section. First, when a program is terminated due to inadequate continuation funding, important program goals often are not achieved. Thus, the original grant is not leveraged for long-term success. Second, most funders give considerable attention to this section, because like you, they don't want your project to fail once the initial grant is used up. Some details should be given in the future funding section on the ways fundraising will be expanded to include the new project and who will assume responsibility.

In a *capital/equipment proposal*—that is, a proposal to obtain funding for major equipment purchases or building renovations and expansions—grantmakers need to know what else the organization will need to operate the equipment, what additional costs will be incurred to maintain a new building, and the sources of funding to increase service if building expansion will result in program expansion.

Future funding can come from the following sources:

- *Continuation grants from foundations and corporations:* Nonprofits can seek continuing support from those foundations and corporations that fund ongoing programs.

- *Annual campaigns:* The organization can derive donation revenues from such yearly efforts as membership drives, special events, and gift clubs.
- *Fee-for-service:* If your organization plans to ask clients to pay fees, the fee scale and a revenue plan should be shown. There are two approaches to planning a fee structure for a program: (1) determine a reasonable fee, then determine the donations needed to reach the revenue target; or (2) determine the donations expected for the program, then determine the fees that must be charged to generate the revenue necessary for the project.
- *Sales of items or activities:* The organization can set up a profitable sales program, such as a gift shop or thrift store. In addition, it can sell publications, concert recordings, and educational activities. Profits from these sales might help cover the costs of the project. A clear expense/revenue projection should be given if this route is taken.

An organization with previous successes in funding projects after the life of a grant should describe these accomplishments and demonstrate how the new project will also be funded successfully.

A common error in writing the future funding section is to be too general by indicating that future funds will come from "a variety of sources such as individuals and corporations." Most funders regard such statements with considerable suspicion.

■ Tips for Writing the Future Funding Section

- Even though funders do not always ask for this section of the proposal, it is important to include some information on where money for the project will come from.
- A one-line sentence explaining that future funding will be sought is not enough information for funders.
- The more specific you are in this section, the more confidence you will inspire in your potential funders that the project will continue after they go away.

Use Worksheet 6.1 to begin developing the future funding component of your proposal. Then write your own future funding information using the Sample Future Funding Component. Review your work using the Future Funding Review Questions.

■ Sample Future Funding Component

The Meals Consortium has a strong history of obtaining ongoing funding for Meals on Wheels programs. The social services referral program is expected to have the support of foundations interested in start-up projects for the first two years. In addition to these monies, the development director will increase the amount of unrestricted funds for the consortium through direct mail and the annual special event. During 1993 the growth rate of the individual donor base was 20 percent, and the special event doubled its net income. Efforts are being made to continue this growth in order to use unrestricted funds for the new program.

WORKSHEET 6.1.   Future Funding Questionnaire.

Fill in the appropriate information. Use the filled-out chart on the next page as an example.

RISKS AND OPPORTUNITIES	SOURCES OF FUTURE FINANCIAL RESOURCES	INTERNAL REQUIREMENTS
Continue project?	Sources to be used	Plans that impact the methods
How long?		
Resources (direct and indirect) needed		

WORKSHEET 6.1. Future Funding Questionnaire.

Use this filled-out example to help you complete the questionnaire on the preceding page.

RISKS AND OPPORTUNITIES	SOURCES OF FUTURE FINANCIAL RESOURCES	INTERNAL REQUIREMENTS
Continue project? *Yes*	Sources to be used *County government* *Unrestricted funds from direct mail* *Business contributions*	Plans that impact the methods ■ *Collaborate with existing social services agencies to help provide follow-up and provide direct services to the homebound elderly.* ■ *Use funds from those unrestricted monies raised through the ongoing consortium development program. These are primarily raised by direct mail.* ■ *Obtain funds and in-kind gifts from businesses that provide products used by older individuals.*
How long? *Until no longer needed*		
Resources (direct and indirect) needed *Staffing* *Equipment* *Social services availability* *Clients*		

■ **Future Funding Review Questions**

Do you hope to see the program continue after the initial funding has been exhausted?

If so, does this section present a plan for securing future funding for the program?

Does it discuss future funding strategies and/or earned incomes strategies?

If requesting a multiyear grant, have you shown a decreasing reliance on grant support?

Preparing the Program Budget

This section discusses estimating how much your program idea will cost and introduces you to the key elements of a budget. Examples are used to aid you in defining the elements, and guidelines for budget preparation are provided.

■ The Project or Program Budget

Key to the proposal is the budget for the project or the agency seeking support. If you are seeking operating, or general, support, you should submit the budget for your whole agency along with your request for unrestricted funds. If you are seeking funding for a special project, you will need to develop a budget that shows the expenses and revenue you anticipate for that project. Depending on the funding source, you may be asked for a very detailed budget or a more general outline of income and expenses.

Usually, government funding sources require considerable detail and provide instructions and budget forms that must be used. Foundations and corporations typically require less detail, but they still rely on the budget to help them evaluate the merit of the proposal.

If a funder's guidelines specify a format or form for the proposal budget, be sure to follow the guidelines. By talking with the funder, you may be able to gain additional information, such as whether the funder's guidelines exclude equipment purchases (but permit leasing equipment) or allow only a certain percentage of overhead.

The budget is the plan you have for the project or for your organization, expressed in the language of dollars. The best budgets "translate" the methods section of the proposal into dollars by showing how many staff and volunteers, for example, are needed to implement the plan that has been described earlier in the proposal. Remember, your budget is an *estimate;* it's your best guess of the income and expenses you anticipate will occur.

A budget may include various components:

- *Project or program budget:* The income and expenses associated with the special project for which you are seeking funding
- *Agencywide budget:* The income and expenses projected for the whole organization
- *Budget detail or justification:* More detail on certain income and expense items
- *In-kind contribution budget:* The expected donated goods and services that will be used on the project or in the organization

Not all proposals require all of these components, and the level of detail will vary from funder to funder and from project to project. In a very few cases, a budget may not be necessary if the cost is included in the main body of the proposal, such as a request to buy a specific piece of equipment or to buy twenty-five tickets to a ball game. If you are submitting a proposal for a special project, an agencywide budget should be included as well as the project budget.

■ Steps in the Budgeting Process

To develop the budget component of a proposal for a specific project, follow these steps:

1. Establish the budget period, the length of time the budget covers.
2. Estimate expenses, obtaining cost estimates as necessary.
3. Decide whether and how to include overhead costs.
4. Estimate donated goods and services that will be used.
5. Estimate anticipated revenues for the project.
6. Check to be sure that the budget as a whole makes sense and conveys the right message to the funder.

Establish the Budget Period

Decide how long a period of time the proposal covers, and develop a budget for that length of time. If your proposal is for a six-month project, the budget should show income and expenses for a six-month period. If your proposal is for a two-year project, the budget must show two years' worth of income and expenses.

If project implementation depends on obtaining funding, you may not know whether you will be able to start in May or in November. In such cases, prepare a "budget for six months." Remember that the period for the project budget does not need to match your agency's fiscal year. However, if you are also submitting an agencywide budget, provide the budget for the current or the upcoming fiscal year.

Obtain Cost Estimates and Estimate Expenses

Begin by estimating *direct* expenses: expenses that are directly related to the project and indispensable to it. Direct expenses include the following:

- Program staff salaries and benefits
- Supplies
- Equipment
- Program-related travel
- Program-related rent
- Printing

If you developed a worksheet on methods and timeline as suggested in Step 4, you have already done most of the work estimating these direct expenses. You may need to obtain some cost estimates for unfamiliar or expensive items, such as equipment. At this stage, don't try to squeeze everything down to the last penny; make your best guess regarding how much it will cost to hire a good intake worker or to design and print your brochure.

Decide on Including Overhead Costs

Indirect costs, often called *overhead,* are costs that are shared by all the programs of an organization, such as the cost of the audit, the executive director's salary, general liability insurance, and the copier lease. Indirect costs are the ones that are essential to all programs of the agency but are difficult to assign in specific amounts to any one program.

Because special projects and programs benefit from the overhead of the agency, it is important to include a portion of these costs in the request for funding. There are several approaches to this "recovery of indirect costs," and the guidelines of the funder are the most important criterion in choosing your approach.

Some funders such as government agencies set a maximum allowable percentage for indirect costs. After you have estimated your total direct expenses, you may be able to add a line item such as "Indirect costs at 15 percent of direct costs." In these cases, a budget detail is usually requested that indicates which items are included under indirect costs. For example, if you have included telephone charges as part of the agency's overall or indirect costs, you cannot also include telephone charges as a direct expense.

Most foundations understand that overhead costs are legitimate costs of a project, but they don't want to pay for more than the project's fair share. Foundations typically don't have formal guidelines for a maximum indirect cost rate, but some will allow an amount that seems reasonable. Your research on the funder will help you know what you can include.

HELPFUL HINT

In some cases, it may be easiest to take certain overhead costs and assign a percentage of each to the project as a direct expense. For example, in addition to the expenses that are immediately necessary to the program, you might add 5 percent of the executive director's time, 15 percent of the copier lease, and 10 percent of the audit cost. If each of your projects and programs includes similar items, each will be contributing toward its share of the agency's overall costs. (This approach is often workable only for smaller organizations.)

Estimate Donated Goods and Services

Not all costs of the project will have to paid for in cash. Donated goods and volunteer time are important to many nonprofit ventures. If, for example, you receive a donated computer or have a volunteer receptionist, the costs of the program will be reduced.

Including these in-kind contributions as part of the budget is helpful in several ways. First, the full scope and cost of the project can be seen by the funder. Second, in-kind contributions demonstrate community support for your project and agency. Third, including in-kind contributions in the budget helps remind *you* and the donors and volunteers of the value of their contributions.

In-kind contributions are usually shown as both income and expense at the same levels. If, for example, you receive $3,000 worth of donated food from local merchants, you also "spend," or use, $3,000 worth of donated food. If a volunteer teacher contributes $5,000 worth of her time, you also pay out $5,000 in teaching expense.

Estimate Anticipated Revenues

The project you are proposing may be funded by more than one source, and many funders feel more comfortable funding projects with several funding partners. Some projects will generate income through fees that can help pay for the project's expenses. Other income may include individual contributions, a special event, or grants from other foundations and corporations. Each possible source of revenue for the project should be estimated and included in the budget.

Generally, funders expect to see a "balanced budget" for the project: one in which income and expenses are equal or approximately equal. Most funders are reluctant to support programs that will end the funding period with either a large deficit or a major surplus of cash.

Remember that if you are showing in-kind contributions in your budget, they should be reflected as both revenue and expense. In the budget example given, you can see the in-kind contribution line item under income, and then each contribution also shows in expenses under its corresponding line item.

HELPFUL HINT

If you are sending requests to several foundations, it's usually a good idea to let them know you're doing so. You might say, for example, "In addition to your foundation, this proposal is being submitted to the ABC Foundation and the XYZ Foundation" or "This project has already received a commitment of $25,000 from the LMN Foundation. Consequently, we are asking your foundation for a grant of $35,000, the balance of the foundation grants needed for the project."

Check for Sense

After preparing the initial budget, take a look to make sure that the budget makes sense and corresponds to the methods discussed earlier in your proposal. Make adjustments in income and expense as appropriate. Remember that the budget should not raise any "red flags." Review the budget through the eyes of the individuals who will be reading your proposal. What might not be clear to you? What would raise your eyebrows?

Use Worksheet 7.1. to prepare a budget for your project. Following it is a Sample Budget for the Meals Consortium example in this workbook to show you what the final product might look like. The Budget Review Questions at the end of this section can help point up areas that might need more work.

WORKSHEET 7.1. Revenue and Expense Budget.

	CASH REQUIRED	IN-KIND CONTRIBUTIONS	TOTAL BUDGET
Revenue			
Foundations			
Government			
Corporations			
Individual donations			
Donated printing and supplies			
Volunteer services			
Government			
Total revenue			
Expenses			
Salaries (prorated if less than full time)			
_____			
_____			
_____			
_____			
_____			
_____			
Payroll taxes/benefits (percentage of salaries)			
Bookkeeping contractor			
Total personnel			
Office rent			
Supplies			
Printing			
Utilities			
Telephone			
Copy services			
Postage			
Travel			
Membership dues			
Total non-personnel			
Total expenses			

■ **Sample Budget: Meals Consortium Social Services Referral Program**

	CASH REQUIRED	IN-KIND DONATIONS	TOTAL
EXPECTED REVENUE			
Grants			
Foundations	$75,000		$75,000
Government	$60,000		$60,000
Corporations	$25,000		$25,000
Individual contributions	$47,000		$47,000
Special events (net)	$20,000		$20,000
In-kind donations		$22,000	$22,000
Total revenue	$227,000	$22,000	$249,000
EXPECTED EXPENSES			
Salaries[a]			
Program coordinator	$35,000		$35,000
Social worker I	$30,000		$30,000
Social worker II	$32,000		$32,000
Administrative assistant	$20,000		$20,000
Executive director (part time: $45,000 x 20 percent)	$9,000		$9,000
Benefits[b] (20 percent of salaries)	$25,200		$25,200
Contract personnel	$27,000	$5,000	$32,000
Program services		$9,000	$9,000
Total personnel	$178,200	$14,000	$192,200
Office rent[c]	$7,200		$7,200
Insurance	$1,500		$1,500
Printing	$7,500	$3,000	$10,500
Equipment	$10,000	$5,000	$15,000
Office supplies	$4,000		$4,000
Utilities	$1,000		$1,000
Telephone	$1,000		$1,000
Copy services	$2,000		$2,000
Postage	$9,000		$9,000
Travel[d]	$1,800		$1,800
Membership dues	$500		$500
Total non-personnel	45,500	$8,000	$53,500
Total expenses	$223,700	$22,000	$245,700

[a]A program coordinator is necessary to manage the program and ensure effective delivery of services. The salary is based on the county salary survey, which indicates that comparable positions are paid an average of $32,000 to $40,000 full-time equivalent (FTE) annually plus benefits. The social workers' salaries assume that each person has an M.S.W. degree and experience working with elders. The county salary survey indicates that comparable positions are paid $28,000 to $35,000 FTE annually plus benefits.
[b]Benefits includes employer-paid taxes, health insurance, dental insurance, and long-term disability insurance.
[c]Rent for the office is calculated as 30 percent of total rent.
[d]Two staff members attend the conference of the National Association of Social Workers in Minneapolis.

■ **Budget Review Questions**

Is the budget consistent with the proposal's program plan (methods)?

Is there a budget narrative that explains items that may not be immediately clear?

Does the budget include in-kind revenues and expenses?

Does the budget address the question of how overhead costs will be recovered?

Can you accomplish the intended objectives with the proposed budget?

Writing the Introduction to the Proposal

Once the planning sections of the proposal are drafted, an introduction section should be written. This section of the workbook tells you what should appear in your introduction to help establish your organization's credibility. Using examples and a worksheet, you will be able to develop a strong introduction for your own proposal.

■ Purpose of the Introduction

The introduction component of the proposal is often lengthy, since it must describe the organization and provide assurance to prospective funders that the nonprofit can undertake the proposed project. The introduction also frequently contains a brief description of the proposed project.

The introduction may also be called "Background Information" or "Applicant Description" by prospective funders. Essentially, the same information will be expected, regardless of the title of the component.

The introduction of a proposal should tell the reviewer that the organization

- Is fiscally secure
- Is well managed
- Provides important community services
- Has the respect of the community

The main purpose of the introduction section of a proposal is to establish credibility with your funder. This can be done through quotes and statistics relating to the work of your organization, although these should play a minor role.

Generally, an introduction section of a proposal can make use of a lot of different kinds of information, from organizational history to future plans. What actually gets used in a specific proposal is a question of judgment. The guiding question should be: Will this information help build the case for my organization's qualifications to undertake the proposed program? For example, on a project that involves an innovative approach to working with the homeless, it would be helpful to discuss the organization's history and experience with the homeless and its experience with innovative approaches to a particular issue. In another example, on a highly technical project that involves new ways to access the Internet, past organizational experience in telecommunications and the qualifications of specific staff members would be very supportive of your capability to undertake the proposed project successfully. If you are proposing a collaborative project, you might give an example of other collaborative projects that your agency has participated in.

The introduction component should primarily be a narrative describing the qualifications of the organization. Because it is the first major section of the proposal, it needs to be interesting. Giving a detailed account of your ten-year history may have interest to you, but the funder would probably prefer a summary of the highlights of your history that relate to the project needing funding.

Spending considerable narrative space discussing your organizational structure and staffing and board qualifications is also not necessary. There are several supporting documents—such as an organizational chart and resumes of key staff—that may provide this information and give credibility to the organization, but they should be provided in the proposal's appendixes (see Step Ten).

■ Tips for Writing the Introduction

- It is best to begin by explaining when and why your organization got started. Put your mission statement in the first or second paragraph to give the prospective funder a good idea of who you are. Then move away from the philosophy of the organization and begin explaining what you do.
- This section of the proposal can be "boilerplated" for most funders. Slight changes may need to be made to highlight items of special interest to a particular funder.
- Write this section of the proposal after the program planning is finished.
- Use appropriate quotes and data to help your credibility.

Using Worksheet 8.1, develop the introduction component of your proposal. Then write your introduction using the Sample Introduction as a guide. Finally, review your work using the Introduction Review Questions. You should be able to answer yes to each question.

■ Sample Introduction

The Meals Consortium was formed six years ago as a 501 (c) (3) nonprofit, creating a consortium of the five major Meals on Wheels programs in this county. The intent of this cooperative venture of the five agencies is to establish a more coordinated system of meeting the nutritional needs of frail older individuals in the county.

The five agencies that form the consortium are: City Meals on Wheels, Older Adults Services, Seniors Ending Hunger, Valley Meals on Wheels, and the Hunger Program for Seniors. The County Area Agency on Aging provides office and meeting space, telephone, photocopying and mailing services, and limited administrative support.

The Meals Consortium was created to avoid duplication of effort and maximize the effective use of scarce resources among the five major Meals on Wheels programs in this county. The consortium model has resulted in significant cost savings for participating organizations. One example of these savings is that the smaller agencies do not need to pay the high costs of hiring a fundraising staff person who would be necessary to ensure their program growth. Instead, these organizations rely on the Meals Consortium fundraising efforts to assist their programs. There are also considerable cost savings realized through group purchases of items that all the programs use.

The board of directors of the Meals Consortium is comprised primarily of Meals on Wheels program directors, staff members of the County Area Agency on Aging, and interested community members. The current board past-president is a former consumer of Meals on Wheels and is an active community volunteer. The board meets

WORKSHEET 8.1. Introduction Exercise.

Providing information for each of the following sections will help you write your introduction component. Use the filled-out example on the next page to help you complete this exercise.

Name	Accomplishments	Personnel
Location		
Legal status		
Date of beginning		Link to need statement
Mission		
Target population		
Programs		

WORKSHEET 8.1. Introduction Exercise.

Use this filled-out example to help you complete the exercise on the preceding page.

Name	Accomplishments	Personnel
The Meals Consortium	■ *Served more than 255,000 meals in 1993 to over 1,000 frail individuals*	■ *Governing board made up of Meals on Wheels consortium members and interested community members*
Location	■ *Increased the number of persons served in 1993 by more than 5%*	■ *Part-time staff skilled in leadership and fundraising*
Any County, U.S.A.	■ *First Meals on Wheels program consortium in the state*	■ *Volunteers provide help with office work and special events*
Legal status	■ *Strategic planning process completed in 1993*	
Private, nonprofit corporation 501 (c) (3)		
		Summary of need statement
Date of beginning		*The strategic planning process identified that the area of greatest need among the frail individuals served is to be linked up with social services in the county to help them live in their homes.*
1989		
Mission		
Ensure frail seniors can maintain their independence and live with dignity in their own homes		
Target population		
Persons 55 and over who are homebound		
Programs		
Five consortium members provide home-delivered meals		

monthly to review individual organizational efforts and discuss ways of coordinating limited resources to effectively serve their populations.

Two part-time staff manage the fundraising efforts of the Meals Consortium. Administrative support is donated by the County Area Agency on Aging.

The operating budget of the consortium is small to ensure that funds raised go to the five consortium members' Meals on Wheels programs. Finances are managed by the board treasurer, currently a staff person from the County Area Agency on Aging. Overhead expenses are minimal because the County Area Agency on Aging provides office space, equipment, and mailing services at no cost to the program. The fiscal agent for the consortium is the county government. (Please see attached detailed budget for more financial information.)

The effectiveness of the Meals Consortium has resulted in considerable interest from other counties who have more than one Meals on Wheels program. Information is shared and presentations are given to help other groups interested in joining together.

The Meals Consortium agencies serve more than 500 frail elders each day, providing them with hot meals and a friendly visit from a volunteer. In 1993, the consortium members served 255,000 meals to more than 1,200 different elderly men and women. Nearly two-thirds of the meals went to persons seventy-five years of age or older. Half had incomes under $600 a month. Nearly six out of ten lived alone. Minorities made up 37 percent of the total number of individuals served.

In addition to providing hot home-delivered meals to seniors, the consortium members' volunteers who deliver the daily meals provide friendly visits to the sometimes isolated older individuals. These volunteers are an important link to the outside world for the homebound elderly.

By providing home-delivered meals and a friendly visit, the consortium organizations are working to help older individuals retain their independence and live out their lives with dignity in their own homes.

■ Introduction Review Questions

Does your introduction give your organization credibility by stating its purpose, programs, target population and major accomplishments?

Does the introduction section suggest sources of community support for the proposed program?

Will the introduction give readers a sense that the organization is well managed and fiscally secure?

Does the introduction lead nicely into the statement of need?

Writing the Proposal Summary

The proposal is now complete, except for your summary. This component literally summarizes your proposal. In this section of the workbook you will learn what key parts of your proposal should be included in the summary. Using a worksheet and following an example, you will also write a summary for your own proposal.

■ Purpose and Content of the Summary

All proposals of more than five pages in length should contain a summary. Most foundation and government funding sources request one. The summary is a clear, one-page abstract of the proposal. It appears at the beginning of the document, but is written last.

A proposal summary usually contains the following elements:

- Identification of the applicant
- Qualifications to carry out this project
- The specific purpose of the grant
- The anticipated end result
- The amount of money requested
- The total project budget

Each of these elements should be explained in one short paragraph. It is customary to follow the order given above when writing the summary.

A well-written summary will help the reviewer understand the need for the project and the results expected. A poorly written summary will leave reviewers asking why the project is important, which will hurt its chances of being funded. A poorly written summary may be set aside until the reviewer has more time to read through it.

Some writers like to begin their summary section with a statement of the compelling need that the program is addressing. This catches the funder's eye and gives a clear indication of the importance of your program.

The summary is perhaps the most difficult section to write, because it is an exercise in being brief. Writers must catch the essential points of the proposal, set the tone of the proposal, and present the project in a manner that will interest potential funders.

■ **Tips for Writing the Summary**

- Decide what the key points are in each of the sections of the proposal you have written. Only include those key points in the summary.
- Stress those points in the proposal that you know are important to the funder. Make sure the summary highlights your potential funder's priorities.

Complete Worksheet 9.1, using the completed example as a guide. Then write your own proposal's summary. The Sample Summary for the Meals Consortium will help you develop yours. When you are finished writing, review your work using the Summary Review Questions. See if you can answer yes to each question.

■ **Sample Summary**

The Meals Consortium is a consortium of Meals on Wheels programs serving frail older adults in ABC County. The mission of the Meals Consortium is to deliver a coordinated system of home-delivered meals to meet the nutritional needs of homebound seniors.

Recognizing that the target population of homebound older adults needs more than just a hot meal and friendly visit each day, the Meals Consortium is proposing to begin a social services referral program with skilled social workers assessing the nonnutritional needs of the individuals served and making appropriate referrals. The purpose of this new program is to ensure that homebound older adults receive the services they need to maintain their independence and remain in their own home.

Costly institutionalization is about the only alternative to living at home for most of the individuals served by Meals Consortium members. Few individuals have a desire to move to a convalescent home and will struggle to maintain their independence and dignity in their home. With appropriate social services referrals in addition to a good, nutritionally sound diet, frail older adults are able to remain in their homes.

The social services referral program has three objectives: (1) to increase social services referrals and follow-up for individuals served by the Meals Consortium, (2) to increase social services direct care for the most vulnerable older adults served by the Meals Consortium, and (3) to reduce the number of individuals being institutionalized.

Meals Consortium members have served the target population for many years, providing frail older adults with nutritional meals. By forming a consortium six years ago, the Meals on Wheels programs have increased their cost-effectiveness and efficiency. The social services referral program is another step in the consortium's efforts to help individuals maintain their independence.

First-year program costs are expected to be $173,000. This proposal is for $30,000. Remaining funds for the new program will come from a grant from the Area Agency on Aging, from other foundation sources, and from the Meals Consortium annual event.

WORKSHEET 9.1. Summary Questionnaire.

Answer the questions below to identify the main points of your proposal summary. The filled-out example on the next page will help you complete this exercise.

Who are you and what is the mission of your organization?

What is the proposed project (title, purpose, target population)?

Why is the proposed project important?

What will be accomplished by your project during the time period of the grant?

Why should your organization do the project? (Credibility statement)

How much will the project cost during the grant time period? How much is being requested?

Use this filled-out example to help you complete the questionnaire on the preceding page.

Who are you and what is the mission of your organization?

The Meals Consortium is a consortium of Meals on Wheels programs serving frail older adults in ABC County. The mission of the Meals Consortium is to deliver a coordinated system of home-delivered meals to meet the nutritional needs of homebound seniors.

What is the proposed project (title, purpose, target population)?

Recognizing that the target population of homebound older adults needs more than just a hot meal and friendly visit each day, the Meals Consortium is proposing to begin a social services referral program with skilled social workers assessing the nonnutritional needs of the individuals served and making appropriate referrals. The purpose of this new program is to ensure that homebound older adults receive the services they need to maintain their independence and remain in their own home.

Why is the proposed project important?

Costly institutionalization is about the only alternative to living at home for most of the individuals served by Meals Consortium members. Few individuals have a desire to move to a convalescent home and will struggle to maintain their independence and dignity in their home. With appropriate social services referrals in addition to a good, nutritionally sound diet, frail older adults are able to remain in their homes.

What will be accomplished by your project during the time period of the grant?

The social services referral program has three objectives: (1) to increase social services referrals and follow-up for individuals served by the Meals Consortium, (2) to increase social services direct care for the most vulnerable older adults served by the Meals Consortium, and (3) to reduce the number of individuals being institutionalized.

Why should your organization do the project? (Credibility statement)

Meals Consortium members have served the target population for many years, providing frail older adults with nutritional meals. By forming a consortium six years ago, the Meals on Wheels programs have increased their cost-effectiveness and efficiency. The social services referral program is another step in the consortium's efforts to help individuals maintain their independence.

How much will the project cost during the grant time period? How much is being requested?

First-year program costs are expected to be $173,700. This proposal is for $30,000.

■ **Summary Review Questions**

Does your summary clearly identify the applicant(s)?

Does your summary include information regarding the specific need to be addressed and the specific objectives to be achieved?

Does the summary mention the total program/project cost and the amount of funding that is being requested?

Is your summary brief? (approximately one page?)

Putting the Package Together

In this section you will learn the importance of accompanying your proposal with a clear but brief cover letter along with any attachments that funders may request from you.

■ Preparing the Cover Letter

The cover letter is important because it is the first piece of information about your proposal read by a funder. However, it is usually the last piece of the proposal that is written. It should talk about the following:

- The organization making the request
- The support of the board of directors for the project
- The specific financial request being made

The cover letter is usually no longer than one page. The best way to begin the letter is to tell the funder the amount of the request and its purpose. The middle section of the letter explains the proposal's highlights. The end of the cover letter should thank the funder for considering the request and indicate who will be calling to follow up on the request, and when. This is also the place to suggest a meeting between the prospective funder and your organization to answer questions and provide more information. When calling to follow up on the funder's receipt of the proposal, this invitation can be made again. Since the person signing the cover letter may not be the person following up on the request, an indication should be made as to who the organization's contact person will be.

The cover letter should be addressed to the contact person found in the research materials, and it should be signed by the executive director and/or the president of the board of directors.

HELPFUL HINT

Follow up on your proposal within two weeks of sending it. It is important to make sure the contact person actually received your proposal, and it shows your prospective funder your interest.

■ **Sample Cover Letter**

Dr. Lynn Goodperson, Ph.D.
Executive Director
XYZ Foundation
1234 Main Street
Anytown, XY 99999

Dear Dr. Goodperson:

The Meals Consortium is submitting this proposal to the XYZ Foundation for a $30,000 grant to implement a new social services referral program. This new program will enable frail seniors to obtain important social services to help them remain in their own homes.

The board of directors of the consortium believes the social services referral program will provide the five hundred people we serve with important services to help them maintain their independence and dignity. They sincerely hope you will respond favorably to our request for funds.

Our executive director, Ms. Theresa White, will contact you in the next two weeks to see if you have any questions about our proposal. Thank you for your consideration.

Sincerely,

Susan Grantswriter
President, Board of Directors

■ Preparing the Appendixes

In addition to having the proposal's written narrative it is also important to include appendices. The appendixes are not part of the proposal, but they are an important part of the package. Most government and foundation funders give a list of what they wish to receive in the appendixes. Most corporations do not.

If no listing of expected attachments is given, the following should always be included:

- The organization's IRS determination letter
- A list of board members and their work affiliations
- The organization's overall budget for the latest fiscal year
- An organization brochure
- The most current newsletter
- The latest annual report (for those nonprofits that prepare annual reports)
- The organization's long-range plan (if no long-range plan has been prepared, then a list of the annual goals)

- Other funding sources receiving proposals for the project, and the amount of the request
- Letters of support

In addition to these items, a foundation might request profiles of the key staff implementing the proposed project, a list of current funders, and a copy of the latest audit. Corporations are less inclined to want a large appendixes section, but if they have an interest in public exposure, a copy of the organization's marketing plan or copies of media coverage will enhance the proposal.

An appendixes section is also included with a letter proposal. Many of the items mentioned above are generally included in these shorter proposals. Letters of intent should have a reduced appendixes section that includes the IRS determination letter, a list of members of the board of directors, the latest annual report and newsletter, and an organization budget.

■ Proposal Packaging

A clean-looking, neatly packaged proposal gives the impression of a well-organized, successful organization, while an envelope full of pieces of paper with no sense of order gives just the opposite impression.

Time should be taken to make sure the proposal is paginated and that appendixes are clearly marked. Proposals with more than twenty pages should have a table of contents identifying proposal sections. It's also a good idea to precede the appendixes section with a listing of each appendix item.

Only one proposal should be mailed unless more are requested. The original is always sent to the funding source, and if additional copies must be mailed, the original should be clearly marked.

It is recommended that proposals (other than letter proposals with few appendices) should be neatly arranged in folders. The pages of the proposal text should be paper-clipped together (never stapled) and should be in the right-hand pocket of the folder. The appendixes should be in the left side. The cover letter should remain outside the proposal package folder.

While neatness is important to foundations and corporations, a showy, expensive look will not help the success of the proposal. Things to avoid are three-ring notebooks, spiral binders, colored charts and graphs, and laminated or embossed folders.

Following Up
with Funders

Once the proposal is mailed, some follow-up must be done to ensure the funder received the package and to continue the good relationship between organization and funder.

A phone call should be made to the contact person of the funding source by the person in your organization designated in your cover letter. The conversation is to make sure the funder received the proposal and to see if there are any initial questions. During this phone call, you can also find out when a funding decision will be made on the proposal. A face-to-face visit should also be suggested to further discuss the proposal, and a time should be set for that meeting.

If a site visit is required prior to funding, staff members who were instrumental in planning the project and who will be implementing the activities should be available to meet with funding source representatives. Some organizations offer to provide lunch, which gives staff and funders an opportunity to talk more informally. If a meal is provided, it should not be an elaborate, catered event.

If no communication has been received from the funding source in four months or if no information is provided after the expected funding decision date, another phone call should be made to determine the status of the proposal.

Since most organizations send out more than one proposal for the same project, funding sources should be kept informed of changes in the status of other requests for funds. When grants are received, other foundations and corporations receiving proposals should be informed, and they should also be informed if a proposal is denied. As new requests go out for the project, each funding source should receive an update on pending proposals.

Some foundations request that no phone contact should be made with their offices. If this is indicated, then the follow-up calls should not be made. Most corporations and government funders encourage communication about proposals and expect follow-up phone calls.

Once the grant has been received, the organization should properly acknowledge its funder. Foundations and corporations sometimes differ in how they wish to be thanked.

Foundations and corporations expect a thank-you letter, and they want to be kept informed of the project's progress. Even if progress reports are not requested, an update should be mailed at regular intervals throughout the life of the project. Recognizing the funder's generosity in the organization newsletter and annual report is also appreciated.

Large corporations sometimes expect to be thanked in a more public way. While a thank-you letter should always be sent, more recognition may be expected, particularly for large grants. Presentation of the actual check or a representation of it can be made at a board meeting, with photographs taken to send to the press and put in the organization's newsletter. If equipment is being purchased or a building remodeled with a corporate grant, corporate officers should be invited to visit the site for photo opportunities when the project is completed. Corporations are also more interested than foundations in being invited to and publicly recognized at community events. Often, organizations that receive generous corporate contributions publicly acknowledge their donors (for example, with handsome plaques). Smaller corporate gifts should not generate elaborate recognition activities.

Congratulations! You have just developed a great proposal based on the four keys to success discussed in this workbook's Introduction. For a proposal to be successful, it must start with a good idea, which is developed into a good plan. Then it is written clearly and concisely to a targeted funder who has been researched carefully.

Now, using the Special Resource Section at the end of the workbook, you can find out more on how to research funders and develop a successful approach for your proposal. When the proposal has been packaged and mailed out to your prospective funders, return to Step Eleven in the workbook to review the best way to maintain contact with those funders and help move your proposal through the system.

Use the following exercise to make sure your proposal is complete and ready to mail.

WORKSHEET 11.1. Final Proposal Checklist.

Place a check mark next to each step after it is completed.

_____ Determine which project ideas have the best chance of being funded.

_____ Form a planning team that includes clients affected by the project, community leaders, key staff and volunteers, and other organizations with similiar or complementary projects.

_____ Design a program plan.

_____ Conduct thorough research to determine funding sources interested in the project.

_____ Telephone the targeted funding source to request information helpful in preparing the proposal (annual report, grant guidelines, and so on).

_____ Read all funding source materials to ensure their directions are followed while writing the proposal.

_____ Prepare the proposal core components by stating the need or problem being addressed, the objectives and methods to meet the need, how the project will be evaluated and funded in the future, and the budget.

_____ Prepare the final proposal components: the introduction, summary, and cover letter.

_____ Determine those features in the project that may set it apart from others and will appeal to the funder. Make sure those features are highlighted for the funder.

_____ Ensure the proposal is clear and well written by having at least one person review it and give you feedback.

_____ Include the appendices requested by the funder.

_____ Check funder deadlines and the number of proposal copies to be submitted in order to meet their requirements.

_____ Give copies of the proposal to the planning team and other individuals or groups who should be aware of the project.

_____ Make a phone call to the funder within two weeks after mailing the proposal.

Special Resource Section

A. *How to Research Funders*

B. *How to Write a Letter of Intent*

C. *How to Evaluate a Proposal Through the Funder's Eyes*

D. *Bibliography*

E. *Extra Worksheets*

A. How to Research Funders

After the project idea has been determined and the planning phase is under way, research to determine the best funder possibilities can begin. There are several different types of private funders to choose from and a variety of government sources available. This section of the workbook will help you do two things: (1) conduct research to find those funders most likely to give you a grant, and (2) develop a well-targeted approach to help your proposal's chances for success.

Most major metropolitan areas in the United States have a Foundation Center library that has a comprehensive collection of research materials on foundations and corporations. They also carry some information on obtaining support from the federal government. Find out where the closest foundation research library is located. For grantseekers not located close to a Foundation Center library, public libraries and college libraries in most towns usually have some resources for researching funders.

At the end of the research, the proposal writer should know which foundations, corporations, or government sources will have the most interest in receiving a proposal, what the specific interests of each grantmaker are so that the writer can target the proposal to those interests, and whether there is any linkage between the grant-seeking nonprofits and the prospective funder.

HELPFUL HINT

The following list of questions will help you determine funders most likely to fund you:
- Is there an obvious relationship between your project, your organization's goals, and the grantmaker's priorities?
- Can you describe your project in a way that fits the grantmaker's priorities without distorting the purpose of the project?
- Do aspects of your organization and project match any specific requirements of the grantmaker, such as the organization's location, the target population served, or the type of service provided?
- Does the grantmaker give funding at a level that will significantly aid the project in achieving the intended results?
- Does the grantmaker have deadlines and award dates that fit with your schedule for the project?

The following is a good seven-step process for researching potential funding sources using library resources:

1. Determine which funding directories in your Foundation Center library or local library you will be using for research.
2. Determine all the subject areas that the project may fall into. For instance, a proposal seeking funds to begin a senior citizens' meal program would fall into the subject areas of aging and social services.
3. Using the subject index of each directory, look up the subject areas identified for the project and find foundations or corporations in the organization's general geographic area. Also, check the type-of-support indexes for the category of support being sought (continuing, capital, project, and so on). The subject index and type-of-support index can be cross-referenced to determine the best possible matches. You want to find as many potential funders as possible that are close to the nonprofit seeking funds and then move progressively further away as local resources diminish. Write down all the potential funding sources found that are available within a close geographic proximity.
4. Look up, in the directory, each funding source listing found in the subject areas to learn all you can about them. This preliminary research gives you an indication of what funder will have an interest in the project and have the potential of giving funding at the level needed and within the time frame required.
5. For those funding sources that best match the project's funding needs, call for copies of their annual reports and for other materials that will be helpful in preparing your proposal. Foundation and corporation annual reports are important because they generally state the giving interests of the funding sources and list organizations that have obtained grants. If research is being done at a Foundation Center library, information on a foundation funding source can be obtained from its Form 990, usually available on microfiche.
6. With the information obtained from annual reports, Form 990s, and other materials, you can determine how to target the proposal to the interests of the funding source and obtain an idea of how much funding can reasonably be requested.
7. Your organization's board of directors, volunteers, and staff should be made aware of potential funders to determine if they know someone there. If they

---

HELPFUL HINT

In the past several years, many funder data bases have been generated, and it is now possible to do your own research by computer or pay someone to do it for you. There is no question about the time savings this creates for busy people.

To make computer research most effective for you, your subject area should be very narrowly defined. The computer's limitation is that it will give you far too much information (which takes longer to sift through) if you have not been specific, and it may give you too little information if you are not clear about your subject area.

Generally, a computer search is a good place to begin the research process for those individuals who can afford it. However, old-fashioned book research still often proves to be the most reliable in finding the best match.

do, a letter in support of the program can be sent separately from the proposal. While a nonprofit does not have to personally know the individual who makes the funding decision, it is frequently helpful if a good relationship is established.

For those nonprofits that have no library resources available for research, a more creative approach must be taken. The following are some ideas that can be used to build a data base of potential funders:

- Call other nonprofits in the community with similar programs to find out what foundations and corporations are funding them. Get the names of contact people and phone numbers and call the funding sources to obtain copies of their annual reports and funding guidelines.
- Find the names of companies in the local phone book and contact them to determine their giving practices. In this case all research will need to be done over the phone, but the information gathered should be similar to that of library research.
- Become active in chambers of commerce and civic clubs where most members are business professionals and can help identify those companies and foundations in the community that would be interested in proposals.

Preparing a quality proposal with a clear plan to meet a well-identified need is important as the first step to ensuring funding, but just as important is understanding the philanthropic values of foundations, corporations, and government funding sources. There are important differences in approaching foundations, corporations, and government sources. These groups expect some exchange of value (that is, they give funds that are valuable to nonprofits, and they desire something of value in return). Organizations should determine what is of value to each grantmaker they approach.

Foundations, for example, are very clear about their interests, and a copy of any foundation's guidelines will indicate their priorities and what they expect to receive from the grantseeker.

Corporations, on the other hand, are sometimes less clear. Generally, they value an excellent relationship between corporate officials and the nonprofit, or an understanding by the corporation that giving a grant to a nonprofit will build a stronger community.

Government funders state their priorities and often have community advisory groups who help set the priorities and recommend funding. Politics plays an important part in who is and is not given a grant.

Each of these funding groups is discussed below in greater detail to help you research the most promising funders and identify the exchange of value between your organization and your prospective funder.

Researching and Approaching Foundations

When researching funding sources, remember that those foundations most likely to fund a project will fit the following criteria:

- They are interested in supporting programs in your geographic area.
- They are interested in the subject area of your proposed project.
- They have a close personal link to your organization.

There are four different types of foundations: independent, community, operating, and company-sponsored or corporate.

Independent foundations (referred to as private foundations by the IRS) are established by individuals or families and are usually funded either through inherited wealth or wealth accumulated through a business activity. There are three major types of independent foundations:

- *Large multipurpose foundations* often have sizable staffs whose purpose is to assist organizations in preparing proposals, to review incoming proposals, and usually to make recommendations to the foundation board of trustees, which is generally comprised of family members and other individuals. These foundations generally have broad discretionary giving policies, but they usually have specific guidelines that must be followed when approaching them.
- *Special purpose foundations* have defined very specific problems that they wish to address (such as a family creating a foundation to combat AIDS).
- *Small family foundations* generally serve the needs of their local area and may have a broad giving approach or a narrow focus. Smaller independent foundations may have no staff, and the family who established the foundation handles the duties of both staff and trustee.

Community foundations represent the interests and resources of a large number of donors rather than one family. They limit their funding to nonprofits within a narrowly defined geographic area such as a city or region.

In order to make grants, community foundations must acquire donations. These contributions come from a broad base of wealth found within their community. The board of trustees of community foundations usually represents a broad sector of the community, thus helping to ensure their funding decisions cover many areas in need in the community.

Operating foundations are private foundations that use their resources to conduct research or provide a direct service. Although they are frequently listed in research guides, they do not make grants to the general nonprofit community.

Company-sponsored (or corporate) foundations are established by a corporation but tend to operate separately with their own staff. Their boards of trustees are generally members of the corporation. These foundations give grants to nonprofits that are within the geographic interest of company operations, and they will sometimes limit their giving to nonprofits where company employees are actively involved.

Corporate foundations tend to give to a broad spectrum of organizations, although some have specific interests and will establish giving policies that are based on the parent company's interest. For instance, computer companies tend to give to nonprofit organizations requesting funds for projects that utilize computers, and corporations with products for children will be supportive of community programs that assist children.

The Foundation Center reference materials currently track foundation giving in the following categories of support:

- Capital support
- Continuing support
- Endowments
- Fellowships and scholarships
- Matching or challenge grants
- Operating support
- Program support
- Research

Foundations are established to provide philanthropic support to their community. By law, they must give away some of their assets annually. This is one of the major factors that distinguishes foundation attitudes towards giving from corporate attitudes.

Both corporations and foundations want to meet needs in the community, but foundations are generally more philanthropic in purpose than corporations. Foundation representatives in a community sometimes get together to talk about the needs of the area and to determine ways they can meet them through very targeted funding to one nonprofit or a coalition of organizations.

Most foundations are relatively clear about what they wish to fund. Every so often they establish their funding priorities and publish them in some format (such as an annual report or grant guidelines). They are usually clear about the format they wish the writer to follow when preparing the proposal. To find out their funding priorities, proposal format, and deadlines, call the contact person identified when doing research and ask for the following:

- The foundation's annual report
- Grant guidelines
- An application form (if appropriate)
- Deadlines for receiving proposals

Sometimes, this conversation can lead into a brief discussion of the project needing funding, so be prepared to talk about it.

Once the materials are received, it is very important to follow the instructions given for the proposal format and to demonstrate that the project fits into the funder's priorities. (Of course, if it doesn't, then no proposal should be sent to them.)

A common mistake made by writers is to assume the foundation will know the project is a priority and, consequently, take insufficient time to define the project in terms that help the foundation see the fit. If the proposal is presented in a manner that assures the foundation that giving a grant to the project enhances their values, it stands a better chance of being funded. Writers should develop a list of the funding source priorities that seem applicable to the project, and while writing the proposal they should clearly spell out the parts of the project that fit those priorities.

Be careful to avoid the "shotgun" approach of proposal writing. Every foundation has different priorities and some differences in what they wish to see in a proposal. In taking a personal approach with each foundation, much of the core component material may be similar but with different language to highlight foundation priorities, while other sections may differ to a greater degree based on the requirements of each foundation. Organizations that decide to send the exact same proposal and cover letter to lots of foundations are taking the wrong approach and wasting their and the foundation's time.

Nonprofit organizations sometimes feel that if staff or board members do not know trustees of the foundation, then they have no chance of receiving funding, since it is the trustees who make the funding decisions. This is not always true. Making sure the proposal fits the priorities of the foundation and is written in the specified format will give it a very good chance of being funded.

■ Researching and Approaching Corporate Giving Programs

Corporate giving programs are set up within a company, generally as part of the human resources, public affairs, marketing, or community relations departments. One or more company employees provide administrative support for the corporate giving program, and funding decisions are generally made by the CEO or the vice president in charge of the department administering the program. In some cases a committee of key corporate officials is formed to make the grant decisions for the company. These individuals may determine both the monetary and in-kind grants given.

In recent years, corporate giving programs have been cutting back on their cash grants and looking for other ways to support charitable organizations. In-kind contributions to nonprofits have included

- Equipment and furniture
- Professional volunteers providing expertise in their field or serving on a nonprofit's board
- Product donations
- Free or low-cost publicity services

Since non-cash gifts play an important role in most nonprofits, researchers should not overlook this way to obtain corporate support.

In addition, corporate giving programs will sometimes work with nonprofits to develop incentives for consumers to purchase the goods of the corporation that also helps the nonprofit, an arrangement now generally referred to as *cause-related marketing*. An example of cause-related marketing is purchasing checks or credit cards from a bank that gives a portion of the proceeds to a nonprofit. The checks or credit card generally also advertise the name of the organization being assisted.

Corporate giving generally breaks down into the following categories of support:

- Outright gift
- Corporate matching gift
- Use of facilities
- Technical assistance
- Employee volunteers
- In-kind gifts of equipment and materials

Foundations have to give away some of their assets. Corporations do not, since their primary purposes are to supply goods and services and to make a profit, which in turn helps to maintain a healthy economy. Generally speaking, corporations give grants for the following reasons:

- *To create community good will:* Corporations like to be seen as interested in and supportive of the communities where they operate. For this reason, they usually only give grants in communities where they have headquarters and subsidiaries.
- *To support organizations with which they have a strong relationship:* Corporate personnel enjoy feeling personally involved in the nonprofits they support. They may sit on the board of directors or volunteer in some other way, or they may simply be kept informed of the activities of the organization.
- *To support their employees:* Corporations will tend to give donations to organizations where they have employees volunteering, or where employees' families utilize the services of the nonprofit (such as a school or a hospital).
- *For quid pro quo interests:* Corporations often give to organizations that promote the importance of a product made by the corporation. Corporations

generally would like to see some return on their investment in the nonprofit sector. Examples of corporate gain for giving include

Identification with a respectable nonprofit
Increased market share for their product
Increased community visibility

These factors heavily influence corporate giving, and it is important to bear them in mind when preparing grant proposals aimed at corporations. Other ways to enhance the proposal include

- Mentioning linkages that answer the question, What's in it for them?
- Mentioning, in the cover letter, those employees who are volunteers
- Describing ways the organization enhances the quality of life of a company's employees

Companies rarely want a proposal that exceeds three pages in length. An initial phone call should be made to determine the corporation's interest and to request a company annual report and any available grant guidelines.

Unlike a foundation, which has a clearly identified contact person, corporations can have several areas where giving is done. It is essential to identify the appropriate person to approach for your particular project. Keep in mind the following general guidelines:

- The contact person for a corporate foundation is usually identified in their materials.
- The contact person for a corporate giving program may also be found in annual report materials. It is generally the CEO or vice president for human resources, public affairs, or community relations.
- Some corporations don't have an official corporate giving program; they prefer to give grants based on a decision of the CEO and other senior management. These are generally smaller grants, and the CEO usually knows or is personally involved with the organization.

One of the best ways to ensure the success of your proposal is to establish a good linkage with individuals at the corporation. Ways to develop this linkage include

- Meeting the appropriate contact person and establishing a relationship prior to asking for funds
- Sending contact persons the organization's newsletter and brochures as well as press releases announcing new programs or accomplishments
- Sending invitations to attend luncheons or dinners or to participate in special events
- Inviting appropriate company officials to visit the nonprofit organization and meet key staff
- Asking corporations being targeted for solicitation to encourage their top employees to serve on the board of directors or a corporate advisory board

Timing the proposal's arrival at a corporation is also important. When planning the proposal writing schedule, contact a corporation to find out

- If they follow a fiscal or calendar year
- When they plan their grant-giving budgets for the following year

■ When their application deadlines occur
■ When they make funding decisions

Sometimes the best first approach to a corporation is to ask for an in-kind gift rather than a cash grant. Receiving equipment, furniture, or technical assistance helps to build the important relationship that facilitates future attempts to obtain funds.

Once the relationship has been established between the nonprofit organization and corporation, continuation grants are likely as long as the project and the relationship are important to the corporation. The challenge for nonprofit managers is to build and maintain good relationships and to present their project on a continuing basis as one that is valuable to the corporation and to the community.

■ Researching and Approaching Government Sources

Government sources vary widely, from grants given by federal agencies to grants given by local city agencies. Federal grants are usually given in the form of special project funds or categorical grants, which normally go to a state government agency to be distributed to nonprofits within the state. For instance, the federal Department of Health and Human Services has special project funds for AIDS prevention that are given to state governments that can show a need within their state for the funds. The appropriate state agency passes the funds on to local or regional nonprofits who actually perform the service.

In addition to categorical grants, there is federal block-grant money that is given to cities to distribute to nonprofits for capital projects and programs considered of major importance to the cities making the funding decisions. Cities and, in some areas, counties may also have general revenue sharing and discretionary funds that are given to nonprofits. Organizations apply for these funds through a lengthy grant process that must include proposal writing, visits to the local decision makers, and an appearance before the decision-making body to justify the need for the nonprofit to receive the funds.

Researching federal government grant opportunities is generally done by reviewing the *Catalog of Federal Domestic Assistance* published by the General Services Administration. This large book lists more than a thousand federal grant programs. The catalog is now computerized on a system known as the Federal Access Programs Retrieval System (FAPRS). Another useful research tool, the Federal Register, helps the grantseeker keep current on federal grant possibilities. This research tool has been computerized as well. It is possible to obtain abstracts of any Federal Register via the DIALOG system, which is available at most large libraries.

State and local government grant funds are declining as their federal appropriations become smaller. There are still some funds available though, and these sources should not be overlooked. One of the major sources of local grant funding is Community Development Block Grants (CDBG), administered by your city govern-

---

HELPFUL HINT

Call your local congresspeople, state legislators, and city council members to determine what state and local funding is available. They may also be able to help you determine the best approach to take to getting funded.

ment. The staff person in charge of CDBG funds usually can be found by calling the mayor's office in your city.

The *Government Assistance Almanac* and *Catalog of Federal Domestic Assistance* classify federal program assistance as follows:

- Advisory services and counseling
- Direct loan
- Direct payments (grants)
- Project grants
- Sale, exchange, or donation of property and goods
- Use of property, facilities, and equipment

Getting to know influential people in the government agency providing the funds you are seeking is important. The first step to making these contacts is some careful research to decide which government agencies would be interested in funding you. Once that is determined, request information from the department on applications forms, deadlines, estimated sums for new grantees, and a list of past grants. Ask for an informational interview to discuss your project and the agency's potential interest in you. As you develop your proposal (usually from lengthy applications provided for you), call frequently to ask questions and clarify what the funder is looking for. By the time the application is submitted, the agency should be familiar with your organization.

It is also possible to sit on citizen review panels that the government uses to help decide who is funded and who is not. Let the agency know of your interest in doing this and your particular area of expertise. By sitting on one of these panels it is possible to see what the agency's interests are and how decisions are made.

Also, stay in close contact with key government officials. Your application to a government agency should always have letters of support from members of Congress, the state legislature, and your local government.

B. How to Write a Letter of Intent

After the project idea is developed, preliminary research should be done to determine who might be interested in funding the new project. (See Resource A for information on researching funders.)

Some potential funders request a letter of intent to be mailed to them early in your research process so that they can determine if they have an interest in what you are proposing to do. If you are asked to send a letter of intent, it should include the following information:

- Your mission and related programs
- The need you wish to meet
- The outcome you expect from your project
- General details of how you will conduct the project

The following is a sample letter of intent:

Dr. Lynn Goodperson, Ph.D.
Executive Director
XYZ Foundation
1234 Main Street
Anytown, XY 99999

Dear Dr. Goodperson:

The Meals Consortium is submitting this letter of intent to the XYZ Foundation to determine your interest in providing seed funding for our new social services referral program. We are a consortium of the five major Meals on Wheels programs serving the frail elderly in your county. The mission of the Meals Consortium is to develop and coordinate resources for support services to homebound persons, primarily those aged sixty or older.

The board of directors of the organization is comprised primarily of Meals on Wheels program directors who meet monthly to report on individual organization efforts and discuss ways of coordinating limited resources to efficiently assist the member organizations and the populations they serve.

(continued on next page)

In 1993, the consortium programs served 255,000 meals to more than one thousand frail men and women throughout the county. Nearly two-thirds of the meals went to persons seventy-five years of age or older. Half had incomes under $600 a month, and more than half of the individuals lived alone. By providing nutritious meals to homebound individuals, the Meals on Wheels programs are helping to ensure a healthier life-style for each person and providing an alternative to institutionalization.

Our primary goal is to coordinate services for the member Meals on Wheels programs. One need frequently identified by those individuals we serve and by other service providers in the county is for a social worker to ensure the homebound receive the comprehensive care they need to remain in their homes. There currently are no funds available within the separate Meals on Wheels programs to each hire a social worker. By developing a consortium model social services referral program, each program will be served by a coordinated team of professionals who will assess the needs of the homebound elderly and arrange appropriate services.

Our proposal to the XYZ Foundation would be for start-up funds for the social services referral program serving the frail elderly. One hundred percent of the funds received would directly benefit older individuals who need well-coordinated social services to help them live with dignity and in good health in their own homes. Our proposal will request $30,000 to assist in starting the new program.

We look forward to hearing from you regarding our letter of intent. We will contact you in the next few weeks to see if you need more information. If you have any questions about the Meals Consortium, please do not hesitate to contact me at (000) 666–1212 or our treasurer, Joe Smith, at (000) 821–4432. Thank you for your consideration.

Sincerely,

Susan Grantswriter
President, Board of Directors

C. How to Evaluate a Proposal Through the Funder's Eyes

What is it like to decide on funding a proposal? This section of the workbook gives you an idea. As a board member of the We Care Foundation, you will be asked to review the proposal that follows and make a decision regarding its funding. You can take one of the following actions:

- Award a grant in the amount requested
- Award a grant in a different amount from that requested
- Decline to make a grant
- Defer a decision until you have received more information from the applicant

The We Care Foundation is a real foundation that has been given a fictitious name. The foundation agreed to share its guidelines, its board critique sheet, and copies of proposals from its files for this section of the workbook.

Since your staff has done the preliminary screening of proposals, you may assume that the proposal you are reviewing was submitted on time and met other basic requirements.

You will need to consider the following:

- How well the grant request meets your interests and guidelines
- Whether you think the applicant is a credible organization with a competent board, staff, and/or volunteers
- Whether the applicant's plans are feasible, considering the problem or demand to be addressed; the objectives, methods, and evaluation proposed; the amount of money requested; and the total project budget
- How important or compelling the proposed project seems
- Any other biases you or your fellow board members bring to the table

■ Background on the We Care Foundation

The We Care Foundation is a nonprofit grantmaking corporation of a community of religious women in the United States that set aside an endowment to be used to fund projects assisting needy people anywhere in the world. The purpose of the We Care Foundation is to empower people in ministry with the needy to carry on works that improve the quality of life, effect positive changes in attitudes, and change structures that perpetuate inhumane and unjust conditions.

Once a year, the board of directors awards grants to organizations for short-term projects and long-term programs that address

- The food, clothing, and shelter needs of the poor
- The health care needs of the sick
- The education needs of the uneducated
- The survival needs of the displaced
- The advocacy needs of the oppressed
- The conversion needs of the oppressor
- The psychological needs of the suffering
- The spiritual needs of all people

Grants are only made to charitable, nonprofit, nongovernment organizations with proof of tax-exempt status as a 501 (c) (3) organization under the Internal Revenue Code.

Only one request each year from an organization will be accepted. Requests exceeding $15,000 will not be accepted.

Grants are awarded for a one-year period. Grantees may reapply, but the board will not fund the same project or program beyond two consecutive years.

Requests will not be accepted for capital expenditures, tuition, scholarships, fundraising drives, emergency relief, or endowments.

Proposals are limited to six pages (single-spaced), with no cover letter or attachments.

■ **Critique Sheet Used by Board Members of the We Care Foundation**

Credibility Component

_____ Establishes credibility of agency as a good investment
_____ Establishes role of contact person
_____ Establishes qualifications of agency and staff in areas of activities for which funds are requested

Need Component

_____ States a problem of reasonable dimension
_____ Supports a client need with relevant data
_____ Establishes the project/program's current need for funds

Objectives Component

_____ Describes measurable outcomes to be achieved
_____ Appears feasible in light of agency resources
_____ Is achievable within time frame of grant

Methods Component

_____ Describes how objectives will be achieved
_____ Includes staffing, timelines, and client selection
_____ Appears cost-effective

Evaluation Component

_____ Tells process for evaluating accomplishment of objectives
_____ Tells process for evaluating and modifying methods
_____ Tells who will be doing the evaluation
_____ Tells how data will be gathered, analyzed, and reported

Future Funding Component

_____ Tells plan for solvency after grant
_____ Seems probable work will continue beyond grant period

Budget Component

_____ Is complete and accurate
_____ Seems sufficient to cover cost of methods and achieve objectives
_____ Indicates how our funds will be used
_____ Provides information on other sources of income
_____ Will be balanced with addition of our grant

Individual Response:

I support funding: _____ fully _____ partially _____ not at all _____ not sure

Group Response:

$ Requested _____ $ Granted _____ Conditions: Yes _____ No _____

Comments:

■ **Sample Proposal**

This is an actual proposal submitted to the We Care Foundation. The only changes made were in the name of the funding source and the names of the agency and personnel submitting the proposal.

Summary

The Cebola Early Childhood Center is a project that attempts to moderate the negative impact of isolation and poverty on a population of Hispanic preschool children in the mountain village of Cebola, in northern New Mexico. The project, implemented by a well-trained indigenous staff, provides a family-oriented child development program giving these children needed early intervention, supporting the development of self-confidence and high self-esteem, and providing a basic, thorough foundation for future success in school.

Community empowerment and self-determination have always been strong components of this project. Initiated as a cooperative venture among the women in this village, the project was conceived and organized to address the educational needs and the futures of their children to counteract school failure, and to assist in the successful transition to life in the world outside their village.

The women in this village were instrumental in organizing, establishing, and staffing the center, and a local board of women is now directing its operation. The staff has been so deeply committed to obtaining excellence in the early childhood field that they recently extended their education and obtained college-level certification in child development. (Funding permitted the financial support for this training.)

The staff provides an educational program in which their Hispanic traditions and cultural values play a significant part, accomplished by stimulating activities and materials that are organized around a well-developed early childhood curriculum. Ongoing evaluation assures the progress of the children. A close working relationship with the local school district also provides feedback regarding the adjustment and the performance of these children once they enter public schools.

The project is funded mainly through private monies. Fundraising is a continuous, ongoing effort. A grant from We Care will assist in the survival of this project. We are requesting $5,000. This funding will be used for costs related to personnel, non-personnel, and further staff training.

Introduction

This grass-roots program attempts to moderate the negative impact of combined isolation and poverty on rural Hispanic children of preschool age in the village of Cebola, New Mexico. The Cebola Early Childhood Center (CECC) is in its sixth year of operation. It began as a parent-organized cooperative to answer the educational needs of young children in this remote village. In 1984, CECC was given endorsement by the award of CDBG (Community Development Block Grant) monies, through which an early childhood facility was constructed and equipped and local women were employed and trained as early childhood workers. The project has survived on private funding since the termination of the (single year) CDBG grant. It has created services where there were none and provided training and employment to individuals (both women and the elderly) who would otherwise have remained unemployed.

CECC provides family-oriented educational services to preschool children and their parents. The program provides a stimulating environment for children that addresses their intellectual, physical, and social-emotional growth and assures the in-depth mastery of early development stages. The goal of this project is to prepare these children for the future, fostering their self-confidence and high self-esteem as well as providing a basic, thorough foundation for future success in school.

The children who attend the center and participate in a child development program are supervised by trained paraprofessionals. Training for these women, who are indigenous to the village of Cebola, has been extensive. Recently they were awarded their CDA degrees. (The CDA is a nationally recognized credential in child development.) A foster grandparent program is also a thriving component of our project, with half of the teaching staff being senior citizens of the village who are available to the children. The program has been licensed and has been used as a model site, demonstrating excellence both in educational programming and as an early childhood facility. In addition to providing high-quality early childhood education services, the project has been accepted into the State of New Mexico's Child Care Food Program, which provides funding for daily nutritious lunches.

The project director, Becky Smith, is well qualified for her position. She is a lifelong resident of the Cebola community and related to every member of the CECC clientele both through familial and historical ties. She has been trained extensively in child development and has recently earned her CDA degree. Throughout her life she has demonstrated community leadership as well as strong organizational and administrative skills. The contact person, Katherine Jones, is the chairperson of the CECC board of directors and is the key community person governing the project.

Problem Statement

Cebola is a remote village located in Rio Arriba County in northern New Mexico. High unemployment, substandard housing, and low per capita income are characteristic of this region. The population of the area is predominantly Hispanic. Prior to implementation of the CECC program, the community had no educational resources for young children. Through the cooperative efforts of the mothers of this village, CECC emerged as an answer to these needs. It continues to be a grass-roots venture—that is, all staff are members of the community and a parent board is active in directing the center's operation.

The principal problem that this addresses is described best as a problem attendant to isolation and poverty. Isolation and poverty in this rural and predominantly Hispanic region combine to produce a situation for children that is exceedingly difficult to master. Because of the poverty, isolation, and other drawbacks associated with being of a minority group, speaking a different language, and growing up in a rural area, these children will continually face increasingly difficult obstacles throughout their development. School failure has often been the tragic result of this constellation. The CECC program provides a strong educational foundation for these children and an opportunity to deeply master their earliest developmental stages. They are given an "early win," thus setting the stage for self-confidence and future success in school.

CECC exists on a very small and efficient budget. As indicated in the budget, the anticipated financial need for each program year is estimated to be under $25,000. However, because of its geographical isolation, there are few resources available to maintain a program such as this one. We Care funding is needed to assist in this project's survival.

Objectives

The primary objective is to continue to serve an estimated twenty-five children during the coming months with the same high quality we have provided in preceding years. As stated above, the goal of this project is to prepare these children for the future, fostering their self-confidence and high self-esteem as well as providing a basic, thorough foundation for future success in school.

The secondary objective is to continue to serve the parents and/or other family members most responsible for the care of these children with useful types of education, training, and related services that will best serve them in fulfilling their parenting roles.

Methods

CECC serves a population of preschool Hispanic children who reside in the remote mountain village of Cebola, in northern New Mexico. These children begin attending the center very early in their lives, often visiting with their mothers when they are infants and toddlers. Parent involvement is an important component of the program. As the parents attend the center with their child, observe the trained staff interacting with their children, and participate in the child development program, the parents absorb child development concepts in a natural way. An observation room is available for parent use. The staff is also available to consult with parents regarding educational and developmental issues pertaining to their children. An estimated twenty-five children and their families are served each year.

The objectives of this program are realized through the activities of the early childhood program. The center addresses the educational needs of the whole child: the emotional, social, intellectual, physical, and creative aspects of each child's development. The early childhood environment is organized into learning centers, which include (1) the gross motor (large muscle) center, (2) the dramatic play center, (3) the cognitive development center, (4) the constructive play center, (5) the art center, and (6) the book corner. When a child arrives at the program he or she is encouraged to explore and use the different areas according to his or her individual interests. During the course of the day, children also participate in a routine that includes clean-up activities, group activities such as reading and singing together, a nourishing lunch, and outdoor play. Activities are selected to meet the full range of the child's educational needs. Providing a stimulating, well-equipped setting complemented by the skills of a well-trained staff is the key to achieving the project's objectives.

The CECC program is staffed by two early childhood workers. These paraprofessionals are trained in child development and are indigenous to the village of Cebola. They have both recently earned CDA degrees. (The CDA is a nationally recognized credential in child development.) Additional staff support is provided by two senior citizens from the community who function as foster grandparents.

The strong Hispanic cultural elements of the program create an educational climate that enhances each child's self-worth. The indigenous staff is able to provide a program in which Spanish is spoken as the primary language (English is spoken also, but is secondary) and in which Hispanic traditions and cultural values are important components. The child's first school experience is, then, one in which his own culture is valued and functions as a prominent axis of the educational program.

The center operates on a school-year calendar, with one exception. During the coldest winter months, when roads are often impassable, the parents decided that the center would close. This means, essentially, that the center operates each fall from September 1 until Christmas, and each spring from March 1 through early June.

Evaluation

Two forms of evaluation will be conducted for the program. The first form consists of an ongoing evaluation in which the staff meets on a regular basis with a supervisor. The supervisor observes the program and reviews the children's records. Progress notes, assessment forms, and skill charts are used to document and record the educational progress of each child. Meetings between supervisor and staff provide an opportunity for discussion and making decisions regarding needed method modifications. The supervisor is an individual who served as staff trainer during previous program years. Her selection for evaluation is based on her in-depth familiarity with the program and on her extensive training and experience in the fields of child development and education.

The second form of evaluation is an annual process of comparing accomplishments with stated objectives. The El Rito Mountain School District is asked to conduct the annual evaluation. A professional evaluator from the local school district is requested each year because of the school's interest in the program and also because the children attending CECC eventually become students in this district.

Future Funding

As indicated in our budget, our anticipated financial need for each program year is estimated to be under $25,000. Our project survives from year to year through our financial efficiency with the funding we are able to obtain. Each year local organizations within the northern New Mexico territory are approached for support, as are many out-of-state agencies. We plan to continue funding our organization in this manner as long as it is necessary. In the past we have brought our need to the attention of area legislators, and we will continue to do so in the future in hopes that eventually a permanent funding source for this type of activity will be established through state or county government.

Budget

CEBOLA EARLY CHILDHOOD CENTER
JULY 1, 1990 THROUGH JUNE 30, 1991

LINE ITEMS	BUDGET	REVENUE SECURED	OTHER REQUESTS	REQUEST FROM WE CARE
Personnel				
Salaries	$9,072		$6,572	$2,500
Fringe benefits	$1,882		$1,582	$300
Consultant	$3,000		$2,500	$500
Contract services	$900		$900	
Non-personnel				
Telephone	$720		$620	$100
Travel	$1,347		$1,047	$300
Office supplies	$90		$90	
Xeroxing/duplicating	$100		$80	$20
Postage	$120		$100	$20
Maintenance supplies	$90		$90	
Consumable supplies	$300		$240	$60
Educational equipment	$520		$420	$100
Licensing fee	$55		$55	
Insurance	$2,160		$1,760	$400
Utilities	$1,200		$1,000	$200
Nutrition	$1,400	$1,400		
Training				
3 conf. & 1 class	$1,946		$ 1,446	$500
Totals	$24,902	$1,400	$18,502	$5,000
Percentages	100 percent	6 percent	74 percent	20 percent

PENDING SOURCES	PROJECTED DATE OF NOTIFICATION
Public Welfare Foundation	2/90
Sullivan Foundation	2/90
Save the Children	8/90
Rio Arriba County	6/90

Now evaluate this proposal by completing the We Care Foundation critique sheet.

After completing your evaluation of the Cebola Early Childhood Center proposal, you may want to conduct the same kind of review of your own proposal. You should assume your proposal meets the basic guidelines of the funder.

D. Bibliography

■ Guides

Burns, M. *The Proposal Writer's Guide*. New Haven, Conn.: D.A.T.A., 1993.

Hall, M. *Getting Funded: A Complete Guide to Proposal Writing*. Portland, Oreg.: Continuing Education Publications, 1986.

Kiritz, N. *Program Planning and Proposal Writing*. Los Angeles: The Grantsmanship Center, 1980.

Kiritz, N. *Proposal Checklist and Evaluation Form*. Los Angeles: The Grantsmanship Center, 1980.

Read, P. *Foundation Fundamentals: A Guide for Grantseekers*. New York: The Foundation Center, 1986.

■ Directories

The following listing is by no means comprehensive. Its purpose is to get you started in your research.

Corporate Directories

Corporate 500: The Directory of Corporate Philanthropy. San Francisco: Public Management Institute.

Corporate Foundation Profiles. New York: The Foundation Center.

National Directory of Corporate Contributions. New York: The Foundation Center.

The Taft Corporate Giving Information System. Washington, D.C.: The Taft Group.

Foundation Directories

America's Newest Foundations. Washington, D.C.: The Taft Group.

COMSEARCH. New York: The Foundation Center. Computer data base.

Foundation Directory. New York: The Foundation Center.

Foundation Directory Supplement. New York: The Foundation Center. Published annually.

Source Book Profiles. New York: The Foundation Center.

Many states also have grant directories that list foundation funders for the state.

Government Directories

Catalog of Federal Domestic Assistance, 9th edition. General Services Administration. Washington, D.C.: U.S. Government Printing Office.

Federal Access Programs Retrieval System (FAPRS). Washington, D.C.: General Services Administration. Computer data base.

Federal Register. Washington, D.C.: U.S. Government Printing Office. Published daily.

E. Extra Worksheets

WORKSHEET 1.1.   *Proposal Idea Questionnaire.*

1. What new projects (or program expansions) are you planning for the next two to three years?

   Project A:

   Project B:

   Project C:

   Project D:

2. Which of the above projects are compatible with your current mission and purpose? (For those projects outside of your mission, considerable justification will be necessary to convince a funder to support the project.)

Project	Compatible with mission	Not compatible (Check whichever applies)
A		
B		
C		
D		

3. Who else is doing these projects? Is there duplication of effort? Can a partnership be formed that will benefit all organizations concerned with a project?

Project	Duplicate project	Possible collaboration (Check if applicable)
A		
B		
C		
D		

4. What community need does each of your projects address?

Project	Need addressed
A	
B	
C	
D	

5. What members of your community—including civic leaders, political figures, the media, and your own clients—support each project?

Project	Supporters
A	
B	
C	
D	

6. Does your organization currently have the expertise to undertake each project? Will new staff be necessary? Can the organization manage growth in personnel effectively?

WORKSHEET 2.1. Statement of Need Questionnaire.

WHO? WHERE? WHEN?	WHAT? WHY?	EVIDENCE OF PROBLEM	SO WHAT?
Who are the people with the need?	What is the need?	What evidence do you have to support your claim?	What are the consequences of meeting the need?
Where are the people?			
When is the need evident?			
	Why does this need occur?		How is the need linked to your organization?

WORKSHEET 3.1. Goals and Objectives Exercise.

Write your objectives by using the following worksheet to help you focus on outcomes. Start by indicating the goal of the program, and then describe the objectives that tie to the goal. You may have more than one goal (use separate sheets for each goal). You should limit your objectives to one to four per goal.

GOAL: _____

	OBJECTIVE ONE	OBJECTIVE TWO	OBJECTIVE THREE	OBJECTIVE FOUR
Area of change				
Target population				
Direction of change				
Time frame				
Degree of change				

Standard Form for Objective Statements: to (direction of change) + (area of change) + (target population) + (degree of change) + (time frame).

WORKSHEET 4.1. Methods Exercise.

List the key elements of your planned program. Then write a methods section for your proposal.

TASKS/SUBTASKS	RESOURCES NEEDED	START AND FINISH DATES

WORKSHEET 5.1. Identify Your Program Elements.

1. What are the inputs for your program?

2. What are the throughputs? (You may have answered this question with your proposal methods from the previous exercise.)

3. What are the outputs of your program?

4. What are the outcomes?

5. What are the impacts?

WORKSHEET 5.2. Evaluation Planning Questions.

Answer the following questions to plan your evaluation.

1. What questions will your evaluation activities seek to answer?

2. What are the specific evaluation plans and time frames?

   What kinds of data will be collected?

   At what points?

   Using what strategies or instruments?

   Using what comparison group or baseline, if any?

3. If you intend to use your study on a sample of participants, how will this sample be constructed?

4. What procedures will you use to determine whether the program was implemented as planned?

5. Who will conduct the evaluation?

6. Who will receive the reports?

WORKSHEET 6.1. Future Funding Questionnaire.

Fill in the appropriate information.

RISKS AND OPPORTUNITIES	SOURCES OF FUTURE FINANCIAL RESOURCES	INTERNAL REQUIREMENTS
Continue project?	Sources to be used	Plans that impact the methods
How long?		
Resources (direct and indirect) needed		

WORKSHEET 7.1. Revenue and Expense Budget.

	CASH REQUIRED	IN-KIND CONTRIBUTIONS	TOTAL BUDGET
Revenue			
Foundations			
Government			
Corporations			
Individual donations			
Donated printing and supplies			
Volunteer services			
Government			
Total revenue			
Expenses			
Salaries (prorated if less than full time)			
————————			
————————			
————————			
————————			
————————			
————————			
Payroll taxes/benefits (percentage of salaries)			
Bookkeeping contractor			
Total personnel			
Office rent			
Supplies			
Printing			
Utilities			
Telephone			
Copy services			
Postage			
Travel			
Membership dues			
Total non-personnel			
Total expenses			

WORKSHEET 8.1. Introduction Exercise.

Providing information for each of the following sections will help you write your introduction component.

Name	Accomplishments	Personnel
Location		
Legal status		
Date of beginning		Link to need statement
Mission		
Target population		
Programs		

WORKSHEET 9.1. *Summary Questionnaire.*

Answer the questions below to identify the main points of your proposal summary.

Who are you and what is the mission of your organization?

What is the proposed project (title, purpose, target population)?

Why is the proposed project important?

What will be accomplished by your project during the time period of the grant?

Why should your organization do the project? (Credibility statement)

How much will the project cost during the grant time period? How much is being requested?

WORKSHEET 11.1. Final Proposal Checklist.

Place a check mark next to each step after it is completed.

_____ Determine which project ideas have the best chance of being funded.

_____ Form a planning team that includes clients affected by the project, community leaders, key staff and volunteers, and other organizations with similiar or complementary projects.

_____ Design a program plan.

_____ Conduct thorough research to determine funding sources interested in the project.

_____ Telephone the targeted funding source to request information helpful in preparing the proposal (annual report, grant guidelines, and so on).

_____ Read all funding source materials to ensure their directions are followed while writing the proposal.

_____ Prepare the proposal core components by stating the need or problem being addressed, the objectives and methods to meet the need, how the project will be evaluated and funded in the future, and the budget.

_____ Prepare the final proposal components: the introduction, summary, and cover letter.

_____ Determine those features in the project that may set it apart from others and will appeal to the funder. Make sure those features are highlighted for the funder.

_____ Ensure the proposal is clear and well written by having at least one person review it and give you feedback.

_____ Include the appendices requested by the funder.

_____ Check funder deadlines and the number of proposal copies to be submitted in order to meet their requirements.

_____ Give copies of the proposal to the planning team and other individuals or groups who should be aware of the project.

_____ Make a phone call to the funder within two weeks after mailing the proposal.